Praise for Alec Wilkinson and

THE ICE BALLOON

"Fabulous. . . . One feels guilty having so much fun reading about such harrowing voyages."
—*The Boston Globe*

"Fast-moving and often heartbreaking."
—*The Columbus Dispatch*

"Wilkinson's writing is so flawless and engaging that I'd read him on a packed subway at rush hour."
—Sebastian Junger

"Alec Wilkinson is a spare, clear, and lucid writer who works in stylistic simplicity with material that is not simple at all."
—Peter Matthiessen

"*The Ice Balloon* captures a time and place unknown to us now and, in elegant, low-key prose, offers an inspiring narrative of exploration and the indomitable human spirit."
—*Highbrow Magazine*

"Captivating. . . . A thrilling account of a remarkable man."
—*Publishers Weekly*

ALEC WILKINSON

THE ICE BALLOON

Alec Wilkinson began writing for *The New Yorker* in 1980. Before that he was a policeman in Wellfleet, Massachusetts, and before that he was a rock-and-roll musician. He has published nine other books—two memoirs, two collections of essays, three biographical portraits, and two pieces of reporting—most of which first appeared in *The New Yorker.* His honors include a Guggenheim Fellowship, a Lyndhurst Prize, and a Robert F. Kennedy Book Award. He lives with his wife and son in New York City.

Also by Alec Wilkinson

The Protest Singer (2009)
The Happiest Man in the World (2007)
Mr. Apology (2003)
My Mentor (2002)
A Violent Act (1993)
The Riverkeeper (1991)
Big Sugar (1989)
Moonshine (1985)
Midnights (1982)

THE ICE BALLOON

FRI
- Bx
- CVS
- Natalie

SAT
- SC
- Public

SUN
- Apple

- Dorie | Pam | Edy | T.
- Eugene

- Carbone
- Polo Bar
- Snowadays E. 11

THE ICE BALLOON

*S. A. Andrée and
the Heroic Age of Arctic Exploration*

ALEC WILKINSON

Vintage Books
A Division of Random House, Inc.
New York

FIRST VINTAGE BOOKS EDITION, JANUARY 2013

A small portion of this book appeared,
in significantly different form, in *The New Yorker*.

Grateful acknowledgment is made to Viking Penguin for permission
to reprint an excerpt from *Andrée's Story* by S. A. Andrée and Nils Strindberg
and K. Fraenkel, translated by Edward Adams-Ray. Copyright 1930 by Albert
Bonniers Forlag & Hearst Enterprises Inc. Translation copyright © 1930
by Viking Press, Inc. Used by permission of Viking Penguin,
a division of Penguin Goup (USA) Inc.

Images on pages 17, 126, 141, 146, 148, 192, 193, 195, 206, 208,
and 218 are courtesy of the Grenna Museum, Sweden (www.grennamuseum.se)
/ The Swedish Society of Anthropology and Geography. The map on page 49
is courtesy of the Newberry Library, Chicago.

The Library of Congress has cataloged the Knopf edition as follows:
Wilkinson, Alec.
The ice balloon : S. A. Andrée and the heroic age
of arctic exploration / by Alec Wilkinson.
p. cm.
1. Andrée, Salomon August, 1854–1897.
2. Explorers—Sweden—Biography.
3. Balloon ascensions—Arctic regions.
4. Polar regions—Discovery and exploration.
5. Arctic regions—Discovery and exploration. I. Title.
G7001897.W55 2011 910.911'3—dc23 2011025434

Vintage ISBN: 978-0-307-74186-8

Book design by M. Kristen Bearse

Printed in the United States of America
10 9 8 7 6 5 4 3 2 1

For Sara Barrett
and
Sam Wilkinson

THE ICE BALLOON

Chicken, garlic, onions

bacon]

corn
sweet pot
roast ham
s-d tomatoes

- WO
- bfast
- pedi
- old navy
- cheese from murray's

1

In August of 1930, a Norwegian sloop, the *Bratvaag,* sailing in the Arctic Ocean, stopped at a remote island called White Island. The *Bratvaag* was partly on a scientific mission, led by a geologist named Dr. Gunnar Horn, and partly out sealing. On the second day, the sealers followed some walruses around a point of land. A few hours later, they returned with a book, which was sodden and heavy, and had its pages stuck together. The book was a diary, and on the first page someone had written in pencil, "The Sledge Journey, 1897."

Horn rode to shore with the *Bratvaag's* captain, who said that two sealers dressing walruses had grown thirsty and gone looking for water. By a stream, Horn wrote, they found "an aluminum lid, which they picked up with astonishment," since White Island was so isolated that almost no one had ever been there. Continuing, they saw something dark protruding from a snow-drift—an edge of a canvas boat. The boat was filled with ice, but within it could be seen a number of books, two shotguns, some clothes and aluminum boxes, a brass boathook, and a surveyor's tool called a theodolite. Several of the objects had been stamped with the phrase "Andrée's Pol. Exp. 1896." Near the boat was a body. It was leaning against a rock, with its legs extended, and it was frozen. On its feet were boots, partly covered by snow. Very little but bones remained of the torso and arms. The head was missing, and clothes were scattered around, leading Horn to conclude that bears had disturbed the remains.

He and the others carefully opened the jacket the corpse was wearing, and when they saw a large monogram A they knew whom they were looking at—S. A. Andrée, the Swede who, thirty-three years earlier, on July 11, 1897, had ascended with two companions in a hydrogen balloon to discover the North Pole.

Before the twentieth century, more than a thousand people tried to reach the pole, and according to an accounting made by an English journalist in the 1930s, at least 751 of them died. Only Andrée used a balloon. He had left on a blustery afternoon from Dane's Island, in the Spitsbergen archipelago, six hundred miles from the pole. It took an hour for the balloon, which was a hundred feet tall, to disappear from the view of the people who were watching from the shore—carpenters, technicians, members of the Swedish navy who had assisted in the weeks leading up to the launch.

Two years of planning had led Andrée to predict that he would arrive at the pole in about forty-three hours. Having crossed it, he would land, maybe six days later, in Asia or Alaska, depending on the winds, and walk to civilization if he had to. Ideally, he said, and perhaps disingenuously, he would descend in San Francisco. To meet the dignitaries who would be waiting for him, he brought a tuxedo.

Every newspaper of substance in Europe and North America carried word of his leaving. The headline on the front page of the *New York Times* said, "Andrée Off for the Pole." A British military officer called the voyage "The most original and remarkable attempt ever made in Arctic exploration." For novelty and daring, the figure to whom he was most often compared was Columbus.

Then, having crossed the horizon, he vanished, the first person to disappear into the air.

It may be the strangest image in the annals of exploration—a dark gray orb in a white landscape. My wife found it in a slim

English book from 1948 called *Ballooning,* by C. H. Gibbs-Smith, Companion Royal Aeronautical Society. The twenty-eight pages of text refer to prints, woodcuts, engravings, and photographs that range chronologically from "The First Public Balloon Ascent, Annonay, 1783," to "World Altitude Record. 1935." In between are "Death of Madame Blanchard, 1819" (fall from balloon); "An Alarming Experience in Gypson's Balloon, 1847" (lightning); and "The 'Zenith' Tragedy, 1875" (crash). Plate 28 is the orb on its side, with two men contemplating it as if detectives sent to determine the circumstances.

All around the balloon is white from snow and ice, and the sky is white from fog, so there is no horizon, and only a fine line, which the balloon delineates, between the background and foreground. The photograph is not entirely in focus, which makes it appear to be more a print than a photograph, and so somehow obscurely unrealistic, or, on the other hand, realistic in an exaggerated way.

When my wife showed me the image, I assumed it was staged, a Victorian entertainment of some peculiar kind, a lark in an alien landscape, because a balloon couldn't be where this one appeared to be any more than an airplane could be on the moon. And if it wasn't a stunt, I could view it only with a sense of dread for the two men in it. Their craft is wrecked, the landscape is forbidding, and something about the static quality of their forms makes their situation seem utterly hopeless. The caption said, "Andrée's balloon on the ice." Who was Andrée, I wondered? How had he come to be standing beside this ruined contraption, and where was this forlorn place? What had he intended? And what happened to the men in the photograph? Had they made their way safely home? And if they hadn't, how was it that this photograph existed?

2

Except for the bottom of the sea or the center of the earth, the North Pole, at the end of the nineteenth century, was the world's last mysterious destination. For decades before the South Pole was visited—in December of 1911 by Roald Amundsen, a Norwegian—it was known to reside on land, whereas no one knew what lay at the end of where the compass needle pointed. Some thought a temperate sea; some thought more ice; some thought mountains and islands; and, oddly concretizing the inner life, a remnant of early-nineteenth-century believers, called Hollow Earthers, thought a hole there led to an interior world. (The Tropics, on the other hand, while not entirely revealed, had at least been comprehended; no one, for example, thought that they might enclose a frigid desert.)

To go to an unknown place on the earth that might take a year to reach and come back from, using the fastest means possible, is no longer within the capacity of human beings, but between 1496 and 1868 roughly 135 expeditions went to the Arctic, predominantly from Europe. Until 1845 they were mainly looking for a way to get to the East, a trade route, and their attempts were described as voyages of discovery, even though they were made in the service of commerce. The men who took part were passionate to see what no one else had seen. They were filling in the map, not always accurately, but honorably, and one after another, the ice turned all of them back.

A northern passage had become necessary in 1493, when Pope Alexander VI divided the world, East and West, between the Spanish and the Portuguese, leaving the British, less powerful, unable anymore to reach China or India by sailing around Africa.

Following the orders of Sebastian Cabot, a Venetian who, under Edward VI, was "Governour of the Mysterie and Companie of the Merchants Aventurers for the Discoverie of Regions, Dominions, Island, and Places Unknowne," they tried sailing above Russia, a northeast passage, because a map of the period suggested that China and India were closer to England than they actually were. In 1553, Cabot sent three ships to China, two of which got caught in the ice off eastern Lapland, which was uninhabited. According to Sir John Barrow, writing in 1818, in *Chronological History of Voyages into the Arctic Regions,* their crews of about seventy men "perished miserably from the effects of cold, or hunger, or both." The third ship reached a place where, according to Richard Hakluyt, in *The Principal Navigations, Voyages, Traffiques and Discoveries of the English Nation,* published in the early seventeenth century, there was "no night at all, but a continual light upon the huge and mighty ocean." From the White Sea, near St. Petersburg, the captain trekked fifteen hundred miles south to Moscow, met Ivan the Terrible, who was pleased to see him, and established a trade route. In 1556, another English expedition to China made it to Novaya Zemlya, roughly three thousand miles north of the border of Iran and Afghanistan, encountered ice and fog, lost nerve, and turned back. Only one more English expedition went east, in 1580. It consisted of two small ships, one of which was lost.

Martin Frobisher, who made three voyages between 1576 and 1578, was the first Englishman to look for a passage west. Because Magellan had found a way between the Atlantic and the Pacific by sailing south of the Americas, Frobisher believed that he would find one by sailing north. On his first voyage Queen Elizabeth I waved to him from a window as he sailed down the Thames. Weeks later he and his crew met Eskimos in kayaks and from the strangers' Mongoloid features concluded that they were close to China. Five Englishmen went ashore and didn't come back, so Frobisher seized an Eskimo and brought him to England, where he died of a cold. The other artifact Frobisher came home with was a shiny black stone that was somehow taken for evidence of gold. It is not clear how this supposition arose—possibly Frobisher began it cynically as a means of raising money for another voyage—but English speculators embraced it, and Frobisher was sent to get more. Elizabeth named the territory Meta Incognita, which means "worth unknown." Frobisher returned with two hundred tons of the substance.

On his third trip Frobisher left England with fifteen ships and a hundred settlers to establish a mining colony. Three ships were to stay with the colony, and the other twelve were to load up with black stones and return to England. On the way over a storm off Greenland sank the ship that was carrying a lot of their food and the materials for the house that would see them through the winter. When the crew reached shore and took stock of their loss, they realized they couldn't stay. They spent a few days loading up with stones, sailed home, and arrived to learn that the stones from their last trip had been discovered to be iron pyrite, which was not even worth smelting and was eventually crushed for roads. Frobisher was in disgrace, though he revived himself five years later by a marriage that made him rich and by joining up with Sir Walter Raleigh and seizing a Spanish ship, the *Madre de Dios*.

The first man to try to reach the pole was Henry Hudson, in 1607, who believed that the most efficient way to travel to the East would be not to thread one's way among icebound channels and bays of ice, but to go over the top of the world. Hudson was persuaded, as many geographers had been for centuries, that the ice formed only a species of blockade, and that past it was an open polar sea that possibly was temperate. On a voyage in 1610, pressing his crew to continue, he was overthrown. They put him and his son and a few sympathizers in a small boat, and they drifted off, through the bay that had been named for him, and were never heard from again.

After about 1847 most journeys to the Arctic were essentially search parties looking for the British explorer Sir John Franklin, who became the most famous man ever to be lost there. He was fifty-nine when he left England in May of 1845, having been sent to determine whether the part of Canadian coastline that was still unvisited, a little more than three hundred miles, completed the Northwest Passage. He had two ships, the *Erebus* and the *Terror*, which were last seen by a whaler in Baffin Bay, off Greenland, in late July. Franklin had been twice to the Arctic, and one of his voyages had been nearly legendary for its deprivations and suffering, but his third was inept. He sailed into the ice as if a gentleman on a foray into interesting territory, and disappeared.

Many historians think that Lady Franklin sent her husband to the Arctic in late middle age as a means of restoring prestige that had seeped from him (and her). Nevertheless she insisted that the government find him. Over thirty-one years, with public and private money, forty-two expeditions, the bulk of them from England but some from America, went looking for Franklin or for some explanation of why he hadn't come back, then finally for relics of him. More people died in the search than on the expedition. Eventually it was learned from Eskimos and from diaries that were found, and from gravesites and artifacts, that his ships had been enclosed by ice, that he had died early in the confinement, the ships had been crushed, and that every one of his crew, roughly 128 in all, had died in the long retreat, some having practiced cannibalism.

This deeply unwelcome news was brought to England in 1854 by a Scottish explorer named John Rae, who was also a doctor. Eskimos told Rae, through an interpeter, that in the winter of

1850 some of their people had encountered about forty white men who were dragging a boat and some sledges. By means of gestures the white men explained that ice had destroyed their ship, and that they were hoping to reach territory where they could hunt deer. All of them were very thin. They bought seal meat from the Eskimos, camped overnight, and left the following day, heading east toward a river. Months later, by the river, the Eskimos found about thirty bodies and some graves. A day's walk away they found five more bodies. Many of the bodies in both places had been mutilated. As best Rae could, he checked versions of the story against one another and found that they essentially agreed. In his report he wrote, "It is evident that our wretched countrymen had been driven to the last dread alternative as a means of sustaining life." From the Eskimos Rae bought a gold watch, a surgeon's knife, some silver spoons and forks, and a piece of silver plate that was engraved with Franklin's initials.

Rae had meant his account to be private, but it was published in a newspaper, and it outraged Lady Franklin and pretty much the rest of the British, who refused to believe that their naval officers and sailors could have behaved dishonorably. Some people said that the Eskimos probably killed the Englishmen and made up the story. Charles Dickens, in a piece called "The Lost Arctic Voyagers," published in two editions of his weekly magazine *Household Words,* wrote that Rae, while an unimpeachable source, had likely been misled by an interpreter who had been either unskilled or inclined, as were "ninety-nine interpreters out of a hundred, whether savage, half-savage, or wholly civilized," to exaggerate so as to make himself seem more important.

Franklin was a sentimental figure but not a sympathetic one. He and his men had insisted on the rightness of British bearing and cold-weather cunning, and refused to enact any of the widely known practices of the Eskimos whose territories they were crossing. Apparently believing that their ships were invincible and that their tinned food would never run out, they had not included any accomplished hunters among them. The Arctic explorer and scholar Vilhjalmur Stefansson wrote of them in 1938, "One of the most baffling problems of Canadian exploration is how Sir John Franklin and his party of more than a hundred contrived to die to the last man, apparently from hunger and malnutrition, in a district where several hundred Eskimos had been living for generations, bringing up their children, and taking care of their aged." People more favorably disposed to Franklin would respond that the meagerness of the Eskimo's circumstances was proof that game was scarce in the Arctic and that even skillful hunters could not have fed as many men as were left; they had, so to speak, overwhelmed the territory.

Almost no nation managed more, or got beat up worse, in the Arctic than the British, the losses coming partly from a willfully romantic attitude and partly from pridefulness. A famously skilled British sledger of the nineteenth century, Sir Francis Leopold McClintock, who had looked for Franklin, gave a speech on sledging in which he described the British sledger undertaking a journey in the Arctic as characterized by a "strong sense of duty, and an equally strong determination to accomplish it— dauntless resolution and indomitable will; that useful compound of stubbornness and endurance which is so eminently British." Before Franklin disappeared explorers frequently went to the Arctic and had terrible things happen to them, but often they returned and were heroes. After the Arctic erased Franklin and his ships and crew, the British were less keen about what benefits might be had from going there. (By the time the Northwest Passage was completed, in the late nineteenth century, it was useless from being so difficult to navigate. Furthermore, depending on how much ice there was and where it was concentrated, the passage wasn't even in the same place every year.) Almost as a nation the British seemed to feel that the Arctic, having been paid the compliment of courtship, had not played fair.

The difference between the Arctic and the tropics, the other blanks on the period's maps, is one of conception. Each drew a somewhat different type. Discoverers in the tropics were geographers, missionaries, seekers after mineral wealth, or pursuers of stories left in the archives of Spanish exploration about cities of gold. The formidable threats they faced—natives, disease, parasites, unholy heat, antagonistic creatures—were an alliance of resistance. To the European the place was a clotted mass of hazards, a closet in which disaster came at you in waves, whereas the Arctic was the open plain, the desert, the spaces where God and the wild spirits roamed.

In the mind of the eighteenth and nineteenth centuries, the Arctic was a region of severe—even sacred—purity, and the terms of life there were different from those of any more temperate place. In a year, to begin with, it had only one day and one night. Absence defined it. The palette of dangers was reduced to two: cold and starvation. No secondary antagonists such as poison arrows or insects or parasites or diseases intervened, unless in the case of scurvy, which was caused not by an agent native to the ground but by poor nutrition. (Fresh meat, it turned out, protected the Eskimos, but the Europeans relied mainly on lemon juice and the less effective lime juice.)

The path in the Arctic had two ends: arrival or death, which of course was its own arrival. And it was imagined to be the cleanest death, nearly conceptual, a wasting away slowly, an exhaustion relaxing into sleep, it was said; a perishing, an erasure, which was essentially different from a mauling or a withering amid fits of fever or the weakening effects of a larva or a parasite that had worked its way through the bloodstream and the body. A man was believed to have his wits in the Arctic until nearly the end. It was a godly place, fierce and unknowable, the spooky and capacious territory of the imagination. Onto its blackness any idea could be projected. Men who went to the Arctic enraptured, who saw God in the austerity and the other-worldly ice, were often disabused by the experiences they had there, though. A holy-minded American explorer named Charles Hall, viewing the frozen body of a comrade, wrote in a journal, "O, My God, Thy ways are not our ways!"

Finally, while exploration in the tropics might be a treasure hunt, the Arctic offered no riches that could be held in one's hand. In the Arctic what prizes might be obtained would fall mostly to others—the route one found would be traveled. The science one might work would be for selfless gain, and was more likely to be specific than practical, since the conditions of the landscape—a region of ice, not land—were duplicated nowhere else. Certainly one's name would be revered. One would get a statue. One could leave the names of one's family and sponsors and friends on the landscape, although that wouldn't necessarily fill a bank vault.

In 1881 a member of a British Arctic expedition, describing the allure of the frigid places, wrote, "It seems to us certain that the Arctic world has a romance and an attraction about it, which are far more powerful over the minds of men than the rich glowing lands of the Tropics."

The pole was the chaste and pitiless heart of a god-dwelling region. People thought of the tropics and saw golden cities. People thought of the cold territories and shuddered.

3

Why did they go, then, this parade of fanatics heading for the deep places? You have to wonder. What they did was so extravagant that their impulses can't be assumed to have been those of an ordinary citizen, even allowing for the differences between our period and the ones they lived in. It is no observation of my own that the nineteenth century was the last to have been receptive to the enactment of myths, to see the footprints of larger, ineffable beings laid out like dance steps on the map and to feel them wandering through their art and writing. The last to pursue their models and outlines and to feel the rightness of embodying them. Selfless heroism, and the public pursuit and praise of it, reverberates throughout their centuries. The walls of the known, the boundaries, were closer at hand. It was as if the restraints that men felt in sociable life made them feel compelled to rush into the wild.

Who were they? Not a single type but a multiplicity. A procession of thrill seekers, god chasers, romantics, pragmatists, visionary dreamers, nomads, criminals hiding where they thought no one would look, withdrawers from more complicated lives, penitents, mourners, long-shot followers, defeated characters hopeful of redemption, careerists, misfits, and malcontents ill at ease anywhere but the solitary places. Add to them brooders. And self-testers, anxious and feeling vital only when facing a challenge; men whose neurology was sufficiently deadened that only the most profound experiences could stir them. Upright men who adhered courageously to the highest codes of conduct, while marked for death. Devious men who took money from patrons to find Franklin when their intent was to get to the Arctic to find the pole. Ambitious men avid for attention and profoundly receptive to impulse. They set themselves a forbidding task, and came back or didn't, the way heroes do in legends, and in children's books, too.

Very few of them were adequate self-explainers. Someone responding to intuition, to chance and fortune, to sudden insights and epiphanies, often can't explain himself well. Such people act because the gesture feels right, or because they feel provoked, convinced by the obscurity, the persistence, and the vitality of their desires, the self-persuading and incontrovertible correctness of something they see in a vision. "The history of polar exploration is a single mighty manifestation of the power of the unknown over the mind of man, perhaps greater and more evident here than in any other phase of human life," one of them, Fridtjof Nansen, a Norwegian, wrote.

No explorer says, I'll go a little farther than the one who went farthest. He declares for the pole or its equivalent, and he breaks down and turns back or dies sometimes just short of, or just past, where the last mark stood—sometimes merely from luck, bad weather, poor planning. And sometimes determination and a rigorous constitution assert themselves in the vacuum created by hopelessness.

"At least I shall have made my mark on the world," Adolphus Greely, an American explorer, wrote, before leaving on a journey that had a hideous outcome. Nansen's explanation was drawn from that part of the landscape where romance and mysticism merge. During the Arctic night, aboard a ship stuck in the ice, he wrote, "What demon is it that weaves the threads of our lives, that makes us deceive ourselves, and ever sends us forth on paths we have not ourselves laid out, paths on which we have no desire to walk? Was it a mere feeling of duty that impelled me? Oh, no! I was simply a child yearning for a great adventure out in the unknown, who had dreamed of it so long that at last I believed it really awaited me; and it has, indeed, fallen to my lot, the great adventure of the ice, deep and pure as infinity, the silent, starlit polar night, nature itself in its profundity, the mystery of life, the ceaseless circling of the universe, the feast of death, without suffering, without regret, eternal in itself. Here in the great night thou standest in all thy naked pettiness, face to face with nature; and thou sittest devoutly at the feet of eternity, intently listening; and thou knowest God the all ruling, the centre of the universe. All the riddles of life seem to grow clear to thee, and thou laughest at thyself that thou couldst be consumed by brooding, it is all so little, so unutterably little. . . . 'Whoso sees Jehovah dies.' "

Spoken straight from the unconscious, which is wild and ungovernable and used to be called the soul.

4

Flying over the pole in a balloon appears to have occurred to Andrée on the evening of March 16, 1894, after a meeting of the Swedish Anthropological and Geographical Society in Stockholm, when the explorer A. E. Nordenskiöld asked Andrée to walk home with him. In 1878 Nordenskiöld, on the *Vega,* had finally discovered the Northeast Passage. He was interested to know what Andrée thought of using captive balloons—ones tethered to the ground, that is—to rise above the wall of ice surrounding Antarctica and see what lay beyond it. Andrée said, Why not rise above the ice and keep going?

A year later, on February 13, 1895, Andrée described his intentions in an address to the Swedish Royal Academy of Sciences. The following August, in London, at the Sixth International

Geographical Congress, during a morning session devoted to polar exploration, he gave essentially the same speech, called "A Plan to Reach the North Pole by Balloon." He followed General Greely, the American, whose subject was a history of Arctic expeditions, in which he delivered a sort of roll call of nations and names, prefaced by remarks depicting the Arctic as a place where "solitude and monotony, terrible in the weeks of constant polar sunlight," nearly overthrew the mind "in the months of continuous Arctic darkness." It was a territory "of silence awful at all times, but made yet more startling by astounding phenomena that appeal noiselessly to the eye; of darkness so continuous and intense" that a person was led to wonder "whether the world has been cast out of its orbit in the planetary universe into new conditions."

Because I would have chafed at such dramatized talk, however fervent or earned, I imagine Andrée as waiting impatiently to speak. He was thirty-nine, blond, tall, and well built, with wide shoulders and a strong jaw. A woman in the audience described him as "heroic-looking." An acquaintance portrayed him in a letter as "a worthy descendant of the old Vikings." When he felt something passionately, he wasn't above rhetoric, and he liked

the long run-up. In his Swedish accent, words such as "have" came out "haff."

"The history of geographical discovery is at the same time a history of great peril and suffering," he began. "While forcing their way through unknown regions across the vast deserts of Australia, Asia, Africa, the prairies of North America, or through the forests of South America and Central Africa, the explorers have encountered dangers, endured hardships, and been obliged to conquer difficulties, of which no clear idea can be formed by those who have never passed through similar experiences."

In warm climates, however, "nearly every hindrance can be said to contain a means of success." Natives often "bar the way of the explorer, but just as often, perhaps, they become his friends and helpers." Lakes and rivers carried him places; plus he could drink from them and find in them things to eat. In the desert, despite the harsh sun, there could also be "a luxuriant vegetation that serves as a shelter," not to mention people who have been where you are going and can tell you the best way to get there.

In the Arctic, "the cold only kills," Andrée continued. There were "no oases in the icy desert, no vegetation, no fuel," just "a field of ice that invites to a journey," but this field, "covered with gigantic blocks," had proved too daunting to cross. The current might lead a vessel forward, but only into waters filled with ice that crushed ships, and in the high reaches of the Arctic desert, no natives were around to help you. The sun lit one's way in the summer, but it also rotted the ice so that your sledge balked and bogged down and with each step you might sink to your knees. Only by considerable toil could you advance, and then only farther into a landscape that had no comforts or shelter.

"If we further remember that the Arctic explorer can engage in active traveling during a brief season only," Andrée said, "and that during the remainder of the year he is compelled to inactivity under the weakening influence of cold, together with darkness, while he has to resort to the nourishment that is usually unsuitable and often insufficient, and that is always haunted by the consciousness, that the results he can attain will almost inevitably be meagre in comparison with those which can be secured by explorers in other parts of the globe; then it must be admitted that Arctic research offers drawbacks which are materially greater than those encountered by geographical explorers in other places."

Laying out his case, Andrée went on—perhaps incautiously—to malign the sledge, the only means for Arctic travel that had "hitherto been used or even been available for use." Whether drawn by dogs or men, it had failed to carry anyone far enough, "although new efforts to make them a success have repeatedly been made. The fact remains that, in the attempts made for centuries to cross the polar ice, numerous lives and vessels have been lost and large sums of money wasted."

No nation took greater pride in its sledging or its sledgers than Britain, and no nation had lost more of them. Perhaps Andrée was giving the same speech he had given in Sweden, where sledging was not so revered. Possibly he didn't care what the British thought. Or maybe, as his friends sometimes said, he had a tin ear and didn't understand the effect his remarks might have. It requires little of the imagination, however, to hear throats being cleared and feet shuffling.

Nevertheless, Andrée was now at the hinge of his speech. "It would seem," he went on, "as if it were about time to look into the matter carefully, with a view to ascertaining whether there is no other means of transportation than the sledge available for a journey in the regions referred to. We need not pursue the investigation very far to discover such a means, one that appears to be created for the purpose in question. I refer to the balloon."

The perfect and navigable balloon, "which is worshipped because nobody has ever produced one," was not what was needed, he said. The version at hand would suffice—people weren't aware of how suitable it was because, more than seeing its advantages, they were accustomed to noting its defects. "Such a balloon is capable of carrying an exploring-party to the pole and back again," Andrée said. "It is possible, with such a balloon, to cross the Arctic plains."

His purpose declared, he now needed to persuade, and he softened his tone. "To make a journey across the Arctic deserts, is not a purely scientific, but a technical problem." The results of such a voyage were important for science, but the means must be devised by the engineer. A balloon to reach the pole needed to carry three people, he continued, all the instruments they required for scientific experiments, and their food. It should be able to remain aloft for thirty days (the record was fifteen), and, unlike all balloons thus far known, it had to be able to be steered. Last, it had to be inflated in the Arctic.

A larger balloon, with sufficient lift, had been built and displayed in 1878 in Paris at an exhibition, where it made fifteen hundred ascents, each time carrying thirty or forty people, Andrée said. Since then a number of balloons had had the carrying power that the Arctic balloon required. "It is evident that the problem involving the manufacture of a balloon that will satisfy requirement No. 1 has long since been solved by the arts," he said.

Balloons had also been made that retained gas long enough to suggest that a thirty-day flight was achievable. The hydrogen could be manufactured at the launching place or brought in canisters aboard ships. To prevent the wind from interfering with the balloon while it was being filled, a shed could be built as a hangar. Finally, the difficulty in sailing a balloon to a specific destination was that conventional balloons could travel only where the wind blew. A balloonist might take to the air hoping to be carried by currents to where he wanted to land, but the currents could change on him. Andrée announced that he had designed a system using guide ropes and a sail that had allowed his balloon to travel at cross-purposes to the wind.

Next Andrée described the attributes of the balloon he needed. The basket should be "spacious and comfortable," have floats attached, and be hung from the balloon in such a way that it could be disengaged quickly, possibly by pulling a single rope. "The occupants will thus be able to save themselves at sea, when a vessel heaves in sight, by descending to the surface, and, if a heavy wind is blowing, ridding themselves of the balloon." (Such an escape was possible only if a ship was seen. When asked what he would do if his balloon came down in the water with no one around, he said, "Drown.") The balloon should also carry "a sledge, a canvas boat, a tent, arms and ammunition, and provisions for four months, all with a view to making a rescue possible in case of a mishap."

To build the balloon and equip the expedition would cost about thirty-eight thousand dollars. The balloon would travel approximately 250 meters above the ground—below the clouds, that is, and above the fogs. It should start as close to the pole as possible, and as early in July as a brisk and steady south wind arrived. A moderate wind would be better than a powerful one, since the ground would pass in a more regular way, and more of it could be added to the map. "The stay in the unknown regions should be of such long duration as circumstances will permit," he said, "and if chances to visit the surface should occur, they must be improved," meaning acted on.

Being almost finished, Andrée said that he couldn't "help adding a few remarks which will tend to show that not only is it *possible* to cross the Arctics by balloon, but that these regions are particularly well suited for balloon voyages." Obstacles for other expeditions would be advantages for a balloon trip, he said. Since the sun never set during the Arctic summer, he and his companions would be able to take photographs at all hours of territory that had never been viewed, and, since they could always see where they were going, they would not have to tie up at night, "and incur the risk of a heavy gale destroying the harnessed balloon." In addition, the constant sun kept the temperature steady, which helped preserve hydrogen. "In the tropics, on the other hand—for instance, in Central Africa—a balloon would be strongly heated during the day, and considerably cooled at night, whereby great losses of gas and ballast would result."

Furthermore, with the balloon traveling continuously, the trip would take half as long as otherwise. The "glossy" ground without trees to tangle the guide ropes meant that the basket would proceed at a constant altitude, making photographs and scientific measurements easier to manage than if the balloon were passing over a forest. Thunder and lightning, which were common at the equator, and which the balloon, with its ropes wet from rain, would be especially vulnerable to, were almost unknown in the Arctic. Finally, snow, which might collect and sink the balloon, hardly ever fell during the Arctic summer. Any that appeared when the temperature was warmer than freezing would melt, Andrée said, and if the temperature was lower the snow would blow away. What portion settled on the balloon would evaporate, "the evaporation in these regions being very considerable during the season in question."

"The methods heretofore employed to cross the polar ice have not led to the desired result," Andrée said in closing, "and there is no reason to suppose that future attempts of the same nature will be more successful." Undoubtedly, more was to be learned from people who set out in ships and sledges, he conceded, but the knowledge would arrive in increments and only gradually, and a century might pass before the pole was reached. Moreover, the farther the sledges advanced, the more difficult the terrain was likely to be, and the slower their progress.

"With these facts before us, it is only natural to look for other means of accomplishing the difficult task, and every reasonable proposition with a view to solving the problem should be carefully considered," he said. "The solution here proposed, to explore the Arctics by balloon, is not based on obscure theory, but on clear and indisputable facts, which appear to me quite convincing. They teach us—(1) That a balloon can be sent far into the Polar Regions; (2) that it can be kept afloat there a sufficiently long time for the purpose in question; (3) that such a balloon can carry the exploring party there and back; and (4) that many of the peculiarities of the Arctic Regions that have heretofore been a great hindrance in making Arctic exploration, prove to be factors in favour of an expedition by balloon.

"Besides, is it not more probable that the north pole will be reached by balloon than by sledges drawn by dogs, or by a vessel that travels like a boulder frozen into the ice? And can anybody on good grounds deny that it will be possible, by a single successful balloon journey, to acquire in a few days greater knowledge of the geographical aspect of the Arctic Regions than would otherwise be obtainable in centuries?"

5

Among the first in the audience to rise and respond was the president of the Royal Geographical Society, Sir Clements Markham, who had been to the Arctic to look for Franklin. Markham said that clouds might keep Andrée from seeing the ground, or even from knowing whether he was above "land, ice, or snow." Furthermore, unless Andrée descended, he wouldn't be able "to collect natural history specimens," or to take celestial readings to find out where he was. Finally, if the balloon ran into a cliff or an iceberg and was wrecked, how would he get back?

A British explorer of Africa named A. Silva White said that experiments he had conducted with balloons in Scotland had led him to conclude that they couldn't be steered and that Andrée's attempt was "foolhardy, and not one to be seriously discussed at a meeting of this character."

General Adolphus Greely, the American who had spoken before Andrée, added that Andrée's balloon would lose too much gas to complete the trip. If Andrée had solved the problem of permeability, "which has engaged the attention of some of the acutest minds in France and Germany," and to which "money in great sums has been applied," Greely hoped he would share it before he left. Moreover, the southerly winds that might carry Andrée to the pole would converge there and strand him. "As geographers, looking at these things from a practical point of view, and having some knowledge of air and currents," Greely said, "this Congress should not give the weight of their influence or their endorsement to this expedition."

While Andrée listened, he made notes with a pencil. When he returned to the lectern, he said that the discussion seemed to have "wandered somewhat out of the region of the methods by which I propose to make my polar journey." He was aware of how hard flying a free balloon was, he said, but his balloon would control its course by means of guide ropes and a sail. The suggestion that fog might appear in his path had no support. The polar region was about the size of Europe, and as in Europe, there would be fog in some places and not others. He described a trip in the Baltic in which he had controlled his course.

Then he pointed a finger at several explorers. "When something happened to your ships, how did *you* get back?" he asked. Greely, on his expedition a decade earlier, had lost eighteen of his twenty-five men. "I risk three lives in what you call a 'foolhardy' attempt, and you risked how many?" Andrée continued, "A shipload."

He crumpled the paper he had written his notes on and left the stage, arriving at his seat "wiping his brow and taking deep breaths like an athlete," a witness wrote. Meanwhile the audience "cheered until the great hall of the Colonial Institute rang."

6

The first mariners to go toward the North had no idea what they were approaching. Homer described people in *The Odyssey* called the Men of Winter, who lived at the edge of the ocean and never saw the sun. What the Greeks knew of the Arctic they derived from observing that the stars went round a stationary point and that some stars could be seen every night whereas others were only occasional. The two classes were separated by a circular boundary that ran through Arktos, the Great Bear. From astronomical speculations they had deduced that north of the Arctic Circle there was sun at midnight during midsummer, and no sun at midwinter.

The first sailor to advance some ways north was a Greek named Pytheas, who probably lived in the third century BC, about the time of Aristotle and Alexander the Great. He sailed around Britain and six days north to a land he called Thule. What he wrote, which was apparently a geography more than a travel account, survives only in references by other writers, mainly Polybius, and those only brief. It is not possible to tell where Thule was for sure—some people think it was the Shetland Islands, some people think perhaps Iceland—but Pytheas, possibly having encountered ice and fog, wrote that in its vicinity the air, the earth, and the sea all blended, and it was no longer possible to navigate northward.

The next known journeys were made in the seventh and eighth centuries by Irish monks who were seeking a haven. At least some of the monks had followed the flocks of geese that flew over their monasteries. Proof of the monks' visits appears in the form of place-names. Their legacy may be the impression of the Arctic as a sanctified territory, a refuge where a soul might withdraw to cleanse itself.

The Vikings displaced the monks. Among their legends was the visiting of Iceland, which was called Snowland, around 864, by Rabna Floki, which translates as Floki of the Ravens. The mariner's compass hadn't been invented, and fog often shrouded the sun for days, so Floki took three ravens trained to fly toward land (some accounts say two ravens, some say four). When Floki released the first raven, it flew in the direction he had come, leading him to conclude that land was closer behind than ahead. Released farther on, the second raven circled the ship, then also flew toward home. The third one flew forward. Floki spent the winter on Snowland and didn't like it, and is the one supposed to have named it Iceland. After Floki came Ingolf, who with others, in 874, was escaping the rule of the Norwegian king, Hårfager. Approaching the shore of Iceland, Ingolf threw a door over the side of his ship, a Norwegian custom. The gods were supposed to guide the door to a favorable landing, but it drifted out of Ingolf's sight, and he landed on the southern shore of the island. The settlement he established was the island's first permanent one.

The British spent three hundred years looking for the Northwest Passage, dying by degrees, sometimes in big numbers, and usually of scurvy, starvation, and cold. The Arctic scholar Jeannette Mirsky wrote that Arctic exploration from the beginning had been a "series of victorious defeats." Sometimes sandhogs—

the men who build tunnels for trains and aqueducts—describe a task as a man-a-mile job, because a man dies every mile. By victorious defeats, Mirsky meant that while one expedition after another turned back, and many lives were given up, mile after mile of the blankness on the northern map was effaced.

7

After Andrée's speech in London, a lot of explorers and geographers and journalists, offended by the brevity of the voyage he proposed, classified it as a stunt. Arctic exploration was supposed to be a grueling and harrowing journey through the harshest terrain imaginable, conducted sometimes over an interval of years, and occasionally for so long that the explorer and his party were thought to have been lost and often were. The stories the explorers told when they returned were ennobling. The science they did—practically all of it observing and collecting, the categorizing came later—expanded their version of the world. They were naming things for the first time, the way the Greeks named the sky. Their findings provided material for subordinate careers, the ordering and identifying of the natural world based on the artifacts brought back by the people who had been to the far edge of the frontier. Andrée's dash to the pole didn't seem properly respectful. He wouldn't have sufficient time to do science, it was said. His purposes weren't serious, and what value would his accomplishment have? He'd merely own a record.

In interviews Andrée defended himself by saying that he would take plenty of measurements and that the photographs he would add to the map would be invaluable. And what disadvantage could be claimed for seeing a part of the earth that had never been seen before? What he didn't often say is that he would have preferred to cross the Atlantic Ocean, which he regarded as more daunting, but the trip to the pole appealed more to the public imagination and was easier to raise money for. Unlike explorers of the earlier ages and even of his own, Andrée wasn't looking to test himself in a remorseless environment. He didn't see himself as a solitary figure measuring himself against the wilderness and the elements, or as someone trying to wrest from nature its secrets. Or even, as some did, a man in a headlong approach toward the seat of the holy. He was an engineer who wanted to prove the validity of an idea, and he had found a forum in which to enact it.

Andrée was born on October 18, 1854, in Gränna, a small town about three hundred miles southwest of Stockholm, on Lake Vättern. His mother, Wilhelmina, was called Mina, and his father, Claes, was the town's apothecary. They had four other sons and two daughters, with whom they lived above Claes's shop on the main street in the center of town (the building is still there). Mina's father was a mathematics professor, and behind him were three generations of clergymen, some of whom were known for keeping records of the weather. As a child, Andrée was said to have a wide-ranging intelligence, a capacity for asking difficult questions, and to be stubborn. He was fond of games whose outcome depended on solving a problem. His mother noted that if he was treated unjustly by someone, "he spared no effort to pay him back," but "by character and from principle he was magnanimous."

As a boy Andrée built a raft from boards he found, and he and a friend sailed out onto Lake Vättern and had to be rescued when the wind rose. Another time, from a cliff above Gränna, he launched a balloon he had filled with gas, and the balloon landed on the roof of a barn and caught fire. Over the Christmas vacation of 1867, when he was thirteen, he told his father that he no longer cared to study dead languages and that he wanted to be an engineer. He is said to have pounded the table as he spoke.

Andrée's attachment to his mother was profound and only deepened when he was sixteen and his father died. He left money for Andrée to attend the Royal Institute of Technology in Stockholm, where his favorite subject was physics and his closest friendship among the faculty was with his physics instructor, Robert Dahlander. During successive summers Andrée worked as a tinsmith, in a foundry, and in a machine shop, and for two years after he graduated he was a draftsman and a designer in a mechanical works in Stockholm. Through friends he got interested in phrenology, the practice of drawing conclusions about someone's nature and tendencies from the topography of his skull, and while he worked at an engineering firm in Trollhaven, called Nydquist and Holms, he made a phrenological helmet out of brass. It was a half-sphere with screws ascending in rows an inch apart to the crown. It opened into two parts, connected by a hinge, and the screws screwed down to trace the skull's bumps and depressions. Andrée didn't so much believe in phrenology as he was interested in the conclusions phrenologists reached, which he thought sometimes were precisely apt.

In 1876, when Andrée was twenty-three, he went to America to see the Centennial Exposition in Philadelphia, which had been organized to celebrate the anniversary of the signing of the Declaration of Independence. Officially it was the International Exhibition of Arts, Manufactures and Products of the Soil and Mine, and on display were all the world's most prominent new inventions. Absorbed by modernity, he was there when word arrived of Custer's defeat at the Battle of Little Big Horn.

Sailing to America, Andrée had had two acquaintances, his cabinmate, "a young German who was ducking military duty," he wrote in a journal, "and a Swede who claimed to be a pork importer bound for Chicago, but who later proved to be a fugitive." However, "the pseudo pork dealer, who was a good mixer, soon made other friends who were richer than we and with whom he became engaged in gambling. My German cabin mate and I preferred remaining quietly in our berths."

The deserter had brought love letters that he liked to pore through. Andrée had only one book, *Laws of the Winds,* by C. F. E. Björling, which he would read lying on his bunk. One day, reading about the trade winds and struck by their regularity, an idea "ripened in my mind which decisively influenced my whole life," he wrote. This was the thought "that balloons, even though not dirigible, could be used for long journeys. And not only from the Old to the New World, but also in the opposite direction and between the other continents." The German happened to laugh and interrupt Andrée's reverie, but he returned to it and "firmly resolved, when I landed in America, to get in touch with an aeronaut and find out what I could about such balloons as were then manufactured."

In Philadelphia, Andrée went to the Swedish consul to ask for a pass to the fair. The consul said he couldn't give him one, but he could hire him as the janitor at the Swedish Pavilion. He could live upstairs in the pavilion and go anywhere at the fair that he wanted.

Andrée would go to bed at nine and get up at five. One day he made a trip to a river where he picked roses and daisies to press

and send home to one of his sisters. He had only one companion, he wrote her, Plato, "but the best is good enough." It pleased
him that work was honored in America and that the harder
someone worked the better he was treated. At the fair he was
impressed by the machines that printed hundreds of thousands
of newspapers in hours, and the "screws to make pocket watches
so small and delicate that only with a microscope can you see
that they are screws." There was a steam engine "high as a
three-story house," and a cannon weighing "millions of pounds"
that shattered a foot-thick steel plate "as easily as if it were glass."
In New York he had heard they were building "a suspension
bridge over the city, which already cost eighty million crowns,
but it is not ready yet for a long time" (the Brooklyn Bridge was
finished in 1883).

Once in New York and once in Philadelphia, Andrée visited
phrenologists. He presented himself as a tailor, and was told that
he would make an excellent engineer. Also that his determination led people to regard him sometimes as stubborn. His con-
trary temperament made him "quick to avenge insults and repel
attacks." A love for independence and change led to behaviors
that frequently contradicted his feelings. His thinking was
unconstrained by conventions. He could be trusted with "positions that demand masculinity, honor and faith" and was a natural leader: "You win people over to your cause and get them to
sympathize personally with whatever you undertake." Nevertheless, from deep caution, he was "watchful and worried" and
deliberate, and only reluctantly did he trust people. Judgment
and prudence helped him control his fantasies, "however large."
As for his future, twenty years would "pass before you achieve the
highest degree of your spiritual development."

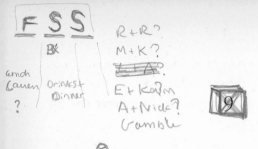

9

Historically the Arctic was congenial to opposites. For some of the ancients, it was both holy and infernal. The devil lived there in a house of fire, a supposition based on a reading of Isaiah 14, which says that Lucifer will "sit on the mount of assembly in the far north." A northerly wind was believed to transmit evil. "The Victorine monk Garnerius says that the 'malign spirit' was called Aquilo, the north wind," Jung wrote in *Aion.* "Its coldness meant the 'frigidity of sinners.' " Jung also wrote that Adam Scotus, a theologian of the twelfth century, believed that "there was a frightful dragon's head in the north from which all evil comes." The smoke that came from the dragon's nose and mouth "was the smoke which the prophet Ezekiel, in his vision of God, saw coming from the north," Scotus wrote.

The anthology of myths and deities and peculiar people assembled about the Arctic by the ancients includes the Arabs in the ninth century who knew about the Arctic from an Arabian traveler named Ahmad ibn Fadhlan. The king of the Bulgarians told Fadhlan that a tribe named the Wisu lived three months north of his country. Their summer nights were not even one hour long. The thirteenth-century Persian geographer Zakariya al-Qazwini says that the Wisu were not allowed to visit the Bulgarians' territory, because wherever they went the air turned cold, even in summer, which killed the Bulgarians' crops. To trade with the Wisu, from whom they mainly got furs, the Bulgarians would go to the border in a cart that was drawn by a dog. It had to be a dog, and not a horse or an ox, because dogs could get a purchase on the ground with their claws—in Wisu there were no trees or dirt or rocks, only ice. The traders would leave their goods on the frontier. When they came back, they would find an item beside their own, and if they liked the trade they would take it. Otherwise they withdrew their item, so they never saw the Wisu or knew what they looked like.

The cold in the north made a fantastic impression on al-Qazwini. Fridtjof Nansen, the Norwegian explorer, in his book *In Northern Mists: Arctic Exploration in Early Times,* quotes his opinion that the northern winter was "an affliction, a punishment and a plague; during it the air becomes condensed and the ground petrified, it makes faces to fade, eyes to weep, noses to run and change color, it causes the skin to crack and kills many beasts. Its earth is like flashing bottles, its air like stinging wasps; its night rids the dog of his whimpering, the lion of his roar, the birds of their twittering and the water of its murmur, and the biting cold makes people long for the fires of Hell." Hell is a complicated notion for people in cold climates. When the Presbyterians went to Alaska in the nineteenth century they told the Indians about the fires of hell that burned perpetually, and the Indians thought it sounded pretty good, so the missionaries had to change hell to a place where it was always cold.

An Arab writer named Shams ad-din Abû Abdallâh Muhammad ad-Dimashqi (1256–1327) described the Far North as a desert with no people in it. It had no animals, either, only great amounts of snow and darkness, and "around it the vault of heaven turns like a stone in a mill."

The Greeks believed that a people named the Hyperboreans lived at the top of the world, beyond the Boreas, the harsh northern wind that issued from a cave. Their territory was a paradise that could not be reached. The Hyperboreans were peaceful and just, they lived in the woods instead of living in houses, they never had wars, and they grew to be a thousand without becoming ill. When a Hyperborean had become tired of life, he or she would put on garlands of flowers, walk to the edge of a particular cliff, and fall into the sea. They cherished Apollo, who could transport to Hyperborea mortals who had lived especially pious lives. To worship him they had a sphere-shaped temple, which hovered on wings. Three brothers who were twelve feet tall were the priests. Every nine years Apollo visited, possibly in a chariot drawn through the air by swans. He played a kind of lyre, called the kithara, and danced for months without resting. When the priests offered their sacrifice and played music, immense herds of swans flew down from the mountains and landed on the temple.

Other ancients thought that a miscellany of oddities and monsters lived in the North. A lost poem from the seventh century BC, called the *Arimaspeia,* was said to have been written by a figure, perhaps mythical, named Aristeas of Proconnesus. Aristeas said that he had traveled to the region of the northernmost people, called the Issedonians. The Issedonians told him that north of them lived the Arimaspians, who had long hair and one eye. North of them were Griffins, which looked like lions and had wings and beaks like eagles. The Griffins guarded the earth's gold and often fought with the Arismaspians, who tried to steal it.

Elsewhere in the North were the Meropians, whose territory shared a border with a country called Anostos, which means "No Return." Anostos had no dark or light, only a reddish fog. There were two streams—the Hedone, which was the stream of gladness, and the Lype, which was the stream of sorrow. Each stream had trees on its banks. If you ate the fruit from the trees by the stream of sorrow, you shed tears until you died. If you ate the fruit by the stream of gladness, your desires were slaked and you got younger, but you lived life backwards and died as an infant.

As for the Romans, Pliny in his *Natural History* described a territory in the north where the snow fell almost constantly and was like feathers. This region had no light, it produced nothing but frost, it was where the north wind lived, and it was cursed. The existence of the Hyperboreans should be accepted, "since so many authors tell us about them," he wrote. Tacitus wrote that the sea in the North was still and sluggish and that the sun in rising from it made a sound that could be heard.

By the fourteenth century, sailors believed that seas in the North had whirlpools so big that traveling into them was like falling into an abyss. In them lived plenty of fantastic creatures. The unknown writer of a thirteenth-century book called *The King's Mirror*, a scientific treatise in the form of a dialogue between a man and his son, said that "the waters of Greenland are infested with monsters." The merman was "tall and of great size and rises straight out of the water." It had a head and shoulders and eyes and a mouth, "but above the eyes and the eyebrows it looks more like a man with a peaked helmet on his head." Its form "looked much like an icicle," in that it narrowed toward its lower half, "but no one has ever seen how the lower end is shaped, whether it terminates in a fin like a fish or is pointed like a pole." The mermaid rarely appeared except before violent storms and was ugly to look at, with a "large and terrifying face."

Instead of whirlpools the author mentions "sea hedges," which are three-sided, "higher than lofty mountains," and box in the sea. "We have to speak cautiously about this matter, for of late we have met but very few who have escaped this peril and are able to give us tidings about it."

Among the region's other attributes were the ice fields on the ocean, which he said were sometimes "as flat as if they were frozen on the sea itself," and icebergs, "which never mingle with other ice, but stand by themselves."

To read these accounts is to feel that the world the explorers were to step into hadn't yet been completely created.

Soon after Andrée got to Philadelphia, he "looked up the balloonist John Wise, an elderly man who had begun his career as a piano polisher," he wrote. Actually Wise had started as a cabinetmaker and had then built pianos. At fourteen, from an article in a German-language newspaper, he got interested in balloons. In his twenties he built one from muslin and varnished it with linseed oil and birdlime, a sticky substance made from tree bark, that was used to trap birds. The mixture, Wise noted, was prone to combust spontaneously.

Wise was also an innovator. He was among the first aeronauts to use draglines as a means for a balloon to maintain a stable height. He also invented the rip panel, which allowed a balloon to deflate quickly and safely for landing. Beforehand a balloonist had to climb through the rigging to the top of the balloon, and with his knees grasp the valve that released the gas. From his weight, the balloon would often turn upside down, which, depending on how hard it hit the ground, might not be so good for the balloonist.

Wise had made roughly four hundred flights "and had had all manner of thrilling adventures," Andrée wrote. "He had flown with them in sunshine, rain, snow, thunder showers and hurricanes. He had been stuck on chimneys, smoke stacks, lightning rods and church spires, and he had been dragged through rivers, lakes, and over garden plots and forests primeval. His balloons had whirled like tops, caught fire, exploded and fallen to the ground like stones. The old man himself, however, had always escaped unhurt and counted his experiences as proof of how safe the art of flying really was.

"In order to convince a few fellow citizens who had been inconsiderate enough to doubt his thesis, Mr. Wise once made an ascent in Philadelphia, and while in mid-air he deliberately exploded his balloon. Then using the remains of the bag as a parachute he landed right in the midst of the doubters. What effect this had on them I do not know, but the old man himself felt better."

Wise believed that the wind blew predominantly from west to east, and with sufficient force and steadiness to transport a balloon carrying people and freight not only across America but also to Europe. Building a balloon to cross the Atlantic was, he wrote, "the dream of my lifetime." The balloon he imagined had a basket shaped like a boat, in case he came down in the water. On the gunwales it had oars and hand-turned propellers. In 1859 Wise started the Trans Atlantic Balloon Corporation with two partners. The balloon they built they flew from Missouri to New York in twenty hours and forty minutes, a record. Two months later, the partners, flying from New York to Canada, crashed in the Canadian woods, and the balloon was destroyed.

In 1873, Wise raised money for a second transatlantic balloon from the *Daily Graphic,* a New York newspaper. This balloon was accompanied by two smaller ones that carried extra gas and could also support someone making repairs to the balloon itself. Wise thought that a crossing to Ireland would take sixty hours and be almost absurdly perilous. "The discovery of the North Pole, which had recently caused Captain Hall's death," he wrote, meaning Charles Hall, who died in 1871 trying to reach the pole, "not to mention the journey of the vessel Polaris"— Hall's ship—"which has just disappeared and probably been lost, is nothing but a pleasure trip compared to this journey through airspace, win or lose." Wise eventually decided that the balloon wasn't substantial enough, and he withdrew. While being filled, the balloon tore and collapsed. A smaller version left for Europe and after three hours crashed in a storm near New Haven, Connecticut.

Wise took Andrée to his shop and showed him "how balloons were cut, sewed together and varnished." When Andrée asked if he might go up in a balloon, Wise "acquiesced immediately, and a short time afterwards informed me that I might accompany his niece, who was to make an ascension a few days later. It was to take place at the city of Huntingdon, Pennsylvania, where the authorities had decided to celebrate the Day of Independence with a balloon ascension."

The evening before, Andrée, Wise, and the niece rode west on a train, with the balloon. When they arrived in the morning Wise said that he needed to rest and gave Andrée the task of filling the balloon, "which I naturally accepted with alacrity." The gas was drawn from a main in the city square, and by five the balloon was full. As Andrée and the niece, dressed as the goddess of liberty, were about to get into the basket, a high wind rose and "the bag collapsed like a rag." The balloon had been torn, and there was not sufficient time to mend it and fill it again. "Thus ended my first attempt to get up into the air."

A few weeks later Andrée heard of a balloon in Philadelphia that would be taking five passengers, and he reserved a place. The ticket, however, cost seventy-five dollars, and he had only fifty, which the owner wouldn't accept. ("To be sure, I had more money," he wrote, "but at the moment it had been lent to a fellow student, who just then was out in the country, painting picket fences at fifty cents a day and board, and thus was in no position to pay me back.")

Not long after that Andrée fell sick with an intestinal complaint that he believed was caused by drinking ice water, but may have been from his living mostly on cake, candy, and ice cream, according to his journals. Having stayed five months in Philadelphia, he went back to Sweden.

Three years later, in May of 1879, Wise wrote a letter to the *New York Times* to say that someone should make a trip to the pole in a balloon. "In the polar summer there is an inflowing current of air that will carry a balloon into the polar basin, if it be kept near the earth, with balance ropes for compensation, to avoid the balloon's rising up into the outflowing current," he wrote.

"It is utterly futile to attempt an ingress by landcraft or watercraft with a handful of men," he continued. "With a well-organized party of a thousand men, moved and stationed at intervals of five miles—say ten men at each station, it may be accomplished. . . . Air-craft is the most feasible—the least expensive, the fewest number of men required, and the shortest time necessary to make the ingress and egress. It is possible to solve the problem within a hundred hours from the time the aerostat is made available. If you deem my suggestions of any value, give the scheme a push, as I am more than convinced that it can be pushed to ultimate consummation through the upper highway."

If Andrée ever saw the letter, he didn't mention it in his writings.

He never saw Wise again either. In September, five months after Wise had written to the *Times,* Andrée "read in the papers that my old friend had gone off on a balloon trip, had been caught in a storm and had never since been heard of." Wise was lost on September 29, in the *Pathfinder,* over Lake Michigan. "For his sake I like to believe that he landed unhurt and that he thereafter encountered obstacles which prevented him from coming home," Andrée wrote.

11

Andrée exemplified a conceit that outlived him—the belief, then nascent, that science, in the form of technology, could subdue the last obstacles to possession of the world's territories, if not also its mysteries. More or less as psychologists were beginning to regard the deeper orders of the mind, this view saw nature as a shadowy chamber of secrets, a vault, that could be illuminated by the new instruments of science. Its banal applications were typified by devices for the home and the factory—the gramophone, the vacuum cleaner, the arc welding machine—that made life easier, and its sinister ones were the innovations in weapons—the machine gun, the torpedo—and their influence on the tactics of war. For all its worldliness it was also an innocent notion, a response to Romanticism, which had influenced earlier ideas about the Arctic.

Andrée might also be said to have believed in a sort of new dismissiveness that held that anything modern was more desirable than a lived-in idea or artifact. The balloon was superior to the sledge and the ship. The encumbrances of the ocean and the land were absent from the air. The sledge and the ship had failed, the balloon and the air were all possibility. He was the first explorer to head toward the pole unaccompanied by Romantic references.

A hallmark of the Romantic tradition was the notion of the "sublime," described by Edmund Burke, in *A Philosophical Enquiry,* which was published in 1757. The sublime was characterized by an astonishment that drove from the mind all other feelings but terror and awe, Burke wrote. This stupefying dread was "the strongest emotion which the mind is capable of feeling." The terror, which was encompassing and prevented reasoning or reflection, was provoked partly by an apprehension of the infinite, and also of the holy. The sublime aroused the deepest feelings the soul could embody, while simultaneously making someone aware that the object which inspired them was a component of a universe that was perhaps largely indifferent, if not unsympathetic, to his well-being both as an individual and a type. Man responded to the sublime because it was glorious—to feel the sublime was to scent the sacred—and because being fitted to feel powerfully, to be profoundly stirred, meant that something of the sublime reverberated within him, otherwise how could he recognize it.

The objects that inspired the sublime were "vast in their dimensions" and "solid, even massive," Burke wrote. Mountains are what he had in mind, the type of towering, pointy, snow-covered peaks that northern Europeans never have to travel very far to stand beneath. When more became known of the immense and remorseless ground of the Arctic, however, with its darkness, its ship-crushing ice, and terrible cold—a place that was both sanctified and antagonistic—it lent itself even more handsomely to the case.

In one of the enduring Romantic novels, *Frankenstein*, a young Englishman named Walton is traveling to the Arctic, as a hobby scientist and discoverer—he hopes to find the Northwest Passage and "the secret of the magnet." He is writing letters to his sister, Margaret, in London. In Russia he writes that a cold wind, which he imagines as coming from the Arctic, has stirred him. "Inspirited by this wind of promise, my day dreams become more fervent and vivid," he says. "I try in vain to be persuaded that the pole is the seat of frost and desolation; it ever presents itself to my imagination as the region of beauty and delight." He pictures it as "a land surpassing in wonders and beauty every region hitherto discovered on the habitable globe," as being "a part of the world never before visited" and "never before imprinted by the foot of man."

The pole during this period was often personified. Vestiges of the romance surrounding it can be found in the introduction to *Arctic Experiences,* an account of an expedition made by the ship *Polaris* toward the pole, published in 1874. "The invisible Sphinx of the uttermost North still protects with jealous vigilance the arena of her ice-bound mystery," it begins. "Her fingers still clutch with tenacious grasp the clue which leads to her coveted secret; ages have come and gone; generations of heroic men have striven and failed, wrestling with Hope on the one side and Death on the other; philosophers have hypothesized, sometimes truly, but often with misleading theories: she still clasps in solemn silence, the riddle in her icy palm—remaining a fascination and a hope, while persistently baffling the reason, the skill, and courage of man.

"Skirmishers have entered at the outer portals, and anon retreated, bearing back with them trophies of varying value. Whole divisions, as of a grand army, have approached her domains with all the paraphernalia of a regular siege, and the area of attack been proportionately widened; important breaches have been effected, the varied fortunes of war befalling the assailants; some falling back with but small gain; others, with appalling loss and death, have vainly sought escape and safety from her fatal toils. Nor has the citadel been won. 'UNDISCOVERED' is still written over the face of the geographical pole."

12

By the time Andrée announced his plan to leave for the pole he was "altogether of Herculean frame," one writer wrote. Another described him as "rather stout in appearance," and as "one of the handsomer men in Sweden." He was six feet tall, with a large nose, "which people in Sweden regard as an augury of success, and a piercing blue-grey eye," which made him seem "cut out for command." A German explorer, Dr. Georg Wegener, met Andrée in London in 1895 and wrote, "The Swedish researcher is a personality cut out of a wood with which world history forms its great men, at the same time daring and balanced, with this strange assurance about progress, with this belief based on the captivating ability to convince, which with all explorers has played the main role, and where the original type is the great, splendid fanatic Columbus." A French geographer especially interested in glaciers, whose name was Charles Rabot, described Andrée as someone who "created sympathy at first sight. I was attracted towards him, at once I felt confidence in him; at our first meeting he gave me the impression of a strong personality." Andrée and Rabot spent an afternoon looking for fossils while Andrée asked about the balloons that had carried the mail during the siege of Paris in 1870 during the Franco-Prussian War. "Everything that I could recollect of these ascensions interested him," Rabot said. "That evening we parted as old friends."

Much of what was written about how Andrée looked and what he was like was written after he had disappeared. He is recalled mostly in tributes, that is, and so he becomes reduced to abstractions and admirable qualities and blurs a little around the edges. He was said to have had few close friends, but among them he was regarded as sociable and devoted. He liked pranks and playing games with children. He had a talent for maxims and penetrating judgments: "Be careful of health, but not of life," he said. Liberals tended to be tranquil because they believed that a moral force lay behind their positions and so were content to see them unfold, whereas conservatives, he wrote, were combative because they regarded themselves as always under attack.

He practiced a precautionary discipline he called self-hypnosis. Someone whose will was strong, he believed, was always liable to coming under its thrall, and "it is therefore essential to direct one's will through daily training towards that which one, through judgment and experience, has found to be sensible and therefore beneficial.

"One masters oneself in the same way one masters others:" he wrote, "by cultivating a keen conception of how one should and should not act." His "coldblooded calmness and realism," wrote a friend, "were not based on a cold temperament, but on his incessant exercise of self-control."

He had no ear for music or writing, or any eye for art. In the portrait of him published in *The Andrée Diaries,* the 1930 account of the voyage and the discovery of the remains, this indifference is described as amounting nearly to "a defect in his character." Friends who persuaded him to go to the opera or an art exhibition "had every reason to repent of their success, for he always managed to spoil their own pleasure by his remarks and criticisms." The writer doesn't mention what those criticisms were, but they were apparently uninformed. When the novelist Selma Lagerlöf was given a prize, Andrée was invited to a dinner in her honor where he was asked if he had read her book, and he said, "No, but I have read Baron Münchhausen"—the German fabulist who had said that he had been to the moon—"and I suppose that it is all the same." An oaf in cultured company is what he sounds like sometimes, but perhaps he was only trying to deflate manners he regarded as pretentious. As for nature, "he displayed a highly developed sense of beauty, and during his many balloon journeys he greatly enjoyed the magnificent scenery."

He seemed to have a kind of intelligence that saw patterns in forms that other people found chaotic, and to be able to hold complicated structures and solutions in his head. He cared deeply about how things went together and how they worked and whether their design was efficient. According to *The Andrée Diaries,* once he decided on an end he did everything he could to attain it. Even so, "no one could weigh every consequence more ruthlessly, more critically than he. He never acted spontaneously, and there was wanting in him the spirit of fresh, impulsive action, but this was compensated for by the sense of security which is conveyed by the actions of an assured, discriminating man. *He embodied, in every respect, the ancient phrase: 'To speak once and stand by one's word is better than to speak a hundred times.'* "

Andrée appears to have been one of those people whose attitudes and habits of mind are literal and firmly formed, so that moving among disciplines is not a matter of broadening oneself by means of new terms so much as applying one's customary judgments to new circumstances. Such a temperament seeks to encounter the familiar and to assess it or deplore its absence, rather than be influenced and possibly enlarged by what it doesn't recognize. It is a commanding, not a humble, state of mind, restless rather than engaged, and capacious more than penetrating. An advantage of it is the capacity to interest oneself in a mulitiplicity of subjects and to arrive quickly at personally satisfying determinations. Andrée's interests were wide-ranging. According to the portrait, he made notes for papers on the influence of new inventions on "every branch of human activity," from "the general development of mankind" to "language, architecture, military science, the home, marriage, education, etc." He wrote about scientific topics, in papers such as "Conductivity of Heat in Construction Material" and "Electricity of the Air and Terrestrial Magnetism." He wrote about social phenomena in others such as "The Education of Girls," and "Bad Times and Their Causes," and about miscellaneous topics such as "The Importance of Inventions and Industry for the Development of Language," and "Directives and Advice for Inventors." He appeared to feel that nothing that interested him was beyond his ability to have an opinion about it.

13

Once Andrée was grown, the only woman for whom he felt a strong attachment was his mother. "Her rich natural endowments, in which good judgment and sharp intellect dominate such characteristics as are commonly called feminine in this day and time, her remarkable will power and capacity for work, as well as her ability to endure and suffer, remind us of the old Norse women," he wrote in a notebook. "Despite her seventy-five years she does not seem old. Her face has few wrinkles. It seems to belong rather to a woman of sixty. The impression of power still unshaken is heightened by her voice which lacks the sentimental, pleading tone one so often finds in older women. Her voice harmonizes with her exterior: firm, strong, almost gruff, but with an undertone of kindliness."

A monument, in other words, erected by a child and tended into adult life—which must have been fatiguing. When Andrée felt himself drawn to a woman, what he called the " 'heart leaves' sprouting, I resolutely pull them up by the roots," he wrote. The consequence was that he was "regarded as a man without romantic feelings. But I know that if I once let such a feeling live, it would become so strong that I dare not give in to it." An acquaintance wrote in a letter that Andrée appeared to have remained a bachelor for the sake of his mother, and for a while they lived with each other. When Andrée was asked why he had never married, he said of any woman who would be his wife that he would not "risk having her ask me with tears in her eyes to abstain from my flights, and at that instant, my affection for her, no matter how strong, would be so dead that nothing could ever bring it back to life."

Figures from history occasionally rise up from the page as if they had merely been waiting, sometimes impatiently, for someone to speak to them. Andrée comes to life a little resentfully, as if interrupted. Through his devotion to his mother he may have been restricted emotionally from mature relationships with women. It is also possible that he was indifferent to showing, or incapable of expressing, any true warmth to another person, except in the narcissistic fashion of a child. His great mechanical abilities and inclinations toward solitude suggest a temperament that does not effortlessly engage in conventional exchanges, one that might easily be confused or defeated or embittered, and might find objects and tasks more agreeable than people. Not all of us want the same things from life. The mainstream forces its preferences on the minority, partly to sustain those preferences, but that doesn't necessarily lend them any substance. Nowhere in Andrée's writings or in the descriptions of him is there an indication of any but a cold-blooded sort of introspection, a capacity for assessing the success or failure of objects and tactics. The territory of feelings seems not to have been hospitable to him.

The only relationship with a woman that Andrée was known to have conducted was an affair with a woman named Gurli Linder, who became in the early twentieth century an admired critic of children's literature. (Linder wrote the portrait of Andrée in *The*

Andrée Diaries.) The affair, which occupied the last few years before he left—Linder in her brief writings on the matter says 1894 was their best and most untroubled year—was conducted so openly that Linder's husband, a professor, asked her to behave with more restraint lest she embarrass him among their friends.

14

In 1875 an Arctic explorer named Karl Weyprecht, who was from Austria-Hungary, suggested that a series of polar outposts be established by various countries so that science could be done and the results of it shared. Weyprecht felt that polar exploration had become glamorized by its rigors and heroes, and by the pursuit of the unknown at the expense of the intellectual work it might better be doing. Weyprecht's plan led, in 1882, to the International Polar Year, in which eleven nations established fourteen outposts, twelve in the Arctic and two in Antarctica. Sweden's outpost was on Spitsbergen. It was overseen by Nils Eckholm, a meteorologist, and, on the recommendation of Professor Dahlander, Andrée's physics professor, it included Andrée, one of whose tasks was to use a device called a portable electrometer to make notations concerning electricity in the air. The delegation arrived in July of 1882. Andrée was second in command.

No photographs I am aware of show Andrée using the portable electrometer, but from the directions for its use, contained in the paper "Instructions for the Observation of Atmospheric Electricity," by Lord Kelvin, published in 1901, it is easy to imagine a solitary figure in the daylight of an Arctic summer standing by a tripod about five feet tall. The tripod is not less than twenty yards from any structure that rises above it ("such as a hut or a

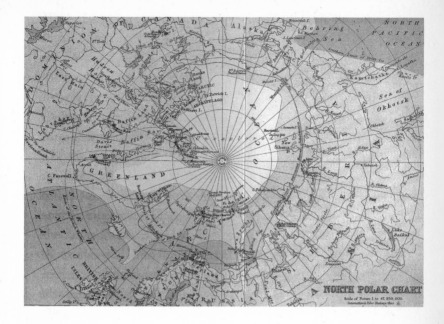

rock or mass of ice or ship," Kelvin wrote). To prevent sparks from static electricity leaping from his fur cap or his wool clothes he has covered the cap and his arms with tinfoil attached to a fine wire he holds in the hand that touches the electrometer. The electrometer has its own metal wire to which a lit match is attached, and while the match burns he makes readings by keeping a hair between two black dots, which he has sometimes to squint to see. Andrée performed the task with such resourcefulness, overcoming technical complications that defeated some of the other nations, and so assiduously—he made more than fifteen thousand observations—that the Swedish findings were considered the best among all the nations.

According to *The Andrée Diaries,* "Andrée also endeavored to find a correlation between the simultaneous variations of aeroelectricity and geo-magnetism. "This has been hard work," he wrote Dahlander, "for it has been necessary to calculate about

5000 values of the total intensity of geo-magnetism." Meanwhile he made notes about the patterns of drifting snow, which he published in 1883 in "Drift Snow in the Arctic." Furthermore, to determine whether the yellow-green tinge that appeared in a person's face at the end of the Arctic winter was a result of the person's skin having changed color in the dark or of his eyes' having been affected by the arriving light, Andrée allowed himself to be shut indoors for a month. When he finally went out, it was clear that the pigmentation of his skin had changed. Before his confinement, Andrée wrote, "Dangerous? Perhaps. But what am I worth?" His diligence did not seem to make him well liked, however. His journals often mention that the others are not doing their work properly or are misbehaving, and that he is the only one comporting himself correctly.

"What shall I do when I come home?" Andrée wrote in his journal. In 1885 he was made head of the Technical Department of the Swedish Patent Office in Stockholm, a position he held until he left for the pole. As a kind of ambassador for science and new technology, he traveled in Europe looking for useful patents—he went to the world's fairs in Copenhagen and in Paris, in 1888 and 1889—especially patents that might reduce drudgery for people who did factory work; he had a social conscience and a conviction that science and new inventions ought to make life less burdensome, that the most useful innovations were applied ones. If people's lives were easier, he believed, they would be happier, and society would be better, with the result that there would be even more innovations. The man he worked for liked him but thought he was stubborn. He was amused at having pointed out to Andrée that while laws and regulations sometimes prohibited innovations they were nevertheless essential, and having Andrée reply that any law that prevented an innovation was wrong. Andrée's personality was forceful, and his approach to social and legal change was not subtle. A few years before he left for the pole, he was a member of the municipal council and introduced a motion that the day for people who worked for the city should be reduced to ten hours from twelve, and that the women's day should be eight hours instead of ten. The proposal failed quickly, and before long, and largely as a consequence, Andrée lost his position on the council.

Between 1876 and 1897 when Andrée left for the pole, the telephone, the refrigerator, the typewriter, the matchbook, the escalator, the zipper, the modern light bulb, the Kodak camera, the gasoline combustion engine, Coca-Cola, radar, and the first artificial textile (rayon) were invented; the speed of light was determined; X rays were first observed and radiation detected in uranium; and Freud and the Austrian physician Josef Breuer began psychoanalysis with the observation in a paper that "Hysterics suffer mainly from reminiscences." Almost quaintly, Andrée embraced modernity by trying to use a half-ancient conveyance in an innovative way.

15

The first balloon plans patented were patented in Lisbon in 1709 by a Jesuit father named Bartolomeu Gusmão. From a balloon, cities could be attacked, he said; people could travel faster than on the ground; goods could be shipped; and the territories at the ends of the earth, including the poles, could be visited and claimed.

Seventy-four years later the first balloon left the ground with passengers, in France. It was built by the Montgolfier brothers, Joseph-Michel and Jacques-Étienne. As children they had observed that paper bags held over a fire rose to the ceiling. Using hot air, their first balloon went up without passengers in the country. Their next went up from Paris with a sheep, a duck, and a rooster, because no one knew what the effect of visiting the upper atmosphere would be, or if there was any air in the sky to breathe. Their third balloon went up with two people. The king wanted the first passengers to be criminals, who would be pardoned if they lived, but he was persuaded that a criminal was unworthy of being the first person in the air, and two citizens went instead.

The hydrogen balloon was developed almost simultaneously by a member of the French Academy named Jacques Charles, who had heard of the Montgolfier brothers' first balloon and mistakenly thought it had used hydrogen. From the place where the Eiffel Tower now is, he sent up a balloon thirteen feet in diameter, also in 1783. Benjamin Franklin was among the audience. The first balloon to go up in England went up in 1784, and the first to crash, when its hydrogen caught fire, crashed in France in 1785.

George Washington watched the first American ascent, in 1793, by a Frenchman who flew from Philadelphia to a town in New Jersey, which took forty-six minutes. Probably the first ascent north of the Arctic Circle was made by a hot-air balloon in July of 1799, built by the British explorer Edward Daniel Clarke, who was visiting Swedish Lapland. He planned the ascent as a kind of spectacular event, "with a view of bringing together the dispersed families of the *wild Laplanders,* who are so rarely seen collected in any number." Seventeen feet tall and nearly fifty feet around, and made from white satin-paper, with red highlights, the balloon was constructed in a church, "where it reached nearly from the roof to the floor." To inflate it Clarke soaked a ball of cotton in alcohol and set the cotton on fire.

The balloon was to go up on July 28, a Sunday, after Mass. The Laplanders, "the most timid among the human race," Clarke wrote, were frightened by the balloon, "perhaps attributing the whole to some magical art." The wind was blowing hard, and Clarke thought it would ruin his launch, but so many Laplanders had showed up he "did not dare to disappoint them." The Laplanders grabbed the side of the balloon as it was filling, and tore it. They agreed to remain in town, with their reindeer, while it was mended. Meanwhile "they became riotous and clamorous for brandy." One of them crawled on his knees to the priest to beg for it.

When the balloon was released that evening, the Lapps' reindeer took off in all directions, with the Lapps running after them. It landed in a lake, took off again, then crashed. The Lapps crept back into town.

Hydrogen balloons are absurdly sensitive to air pressure, temperature, the density of their gas, and the weight they have aboard. Pouring a glass of water over the side of a balloon, or a handful of sand, will make it rise. A shadow falling on it will cause it to descend. A balloon has an ideal (and theoretical) equilibrium, at which it would float indefinitely, assuming it didn't lose gas through the envelope, but that point is impossible to sustain because the balloon's circumstances keep changing. A rising balloon doesn't slow as it approaches equilibrium; from momentum, it continues. Having passed the point of stability, it sheds hydrogen, because the gas has expanded as the pressure of the air has lessened, and the balloon sinks, passing the point on its fall. Shedding the perfect amount of ballast at the ideal rate might settle the balloon exquisitely, but shedding weight also causes the balloon to rise. If it rises too quickly the only corrective might be to release hydrogen, which the pilot would rather retain. Part of the skill of flight, particularly of a flight that is to last a long time, is to manage the altitude with sufficient temperance that little gas or ballast is lost. Enough ballast must be kept to land the balloon properly. Theoretically a balloon might be operated more stably at night, since the temperature does not change as clouds intersect the sun.

Someone traveling in a balloon never feels the wind, or hears it, because he is advancing at the same speed. Early aeronauts, enclosed in silence, used to feel not so much that they were moving as that the land below them was approaching.

16

While Andrée was in Spitsbergen at the Swedish station, making measurements and shut in darkness, the American delegation to the International Polar Year was on Ellesmere Island, opposite the northern end of Greenland, on Lady Franklin Bay. Their camp was about six hundred miles from the pole, and the northernmost of all the nations' camps. The twenty-five members lived in a hut which was sixty feet long and seventeen feet wide and which they had built and called Fort Conger, after a Michigan senator named Omar Conger, who had supported Arctic research. The officers—there were four of them—slept at one end, and the enlisted men at the other. The expedition was to make scientific observations and also to search for the *Jeannette*, which had left to discover the pole in 1879, and disappeared.

The delegation's leader was Adolphus Greely, who had asserted at Andrée's talk in London in 1895 that although Andrée might reach the pole, the Arctic winds, which at that elevation blew only north, would strand him, and then said that the congress ought not to support such a plan.

In *Three Years of Arctic Service,* a fantastically understated title, Greely described some of his comrades at Fort Conger, all of whom had volunteered. Lieutenant Frederick Kislingbury, "in a service of over fifteen years, had a fine reputation for field duty," Greely wrote. James Lockwood "had served eight years, almost always on the frontier, and was highly recommended as an officer of sterling merit and varied attainments.

"Edward Israel and George W. Rice, in order to accompany the expedition, cheerfully accepted service as enlisted men. The former, a graduate of Ann Arbor University, went in his chosen profession as astronomer, while the latter, a professional photographer, hoped to add to his reputation in that art by service with the expedition. Sergeants Jewell and Ralston had served long and faithfully as meteorological observers; while Gardiner, though of younger service, was most promising. Long and hazardous duty on the Western frontier had inured the greater part of the men to dangers, hardships, and exposure."

"Long and hazardous duty on the Western frontier" meant fighting Indians.

In August of 1881, Greely and his men, intending to stay two years, had been left in the Arctic by the *Proteus.* A ship was to visit the following summer to replace anyone who was sick and to leave food and supplies. If ice kept it from reaching the camp, a ship the following year was to stay in Grinnell Sound, about two hundred miles south of Fort Conger, "until there is danger of its closing by ice," the orders said. If the ship had to depart, it was to leave men and food on Littleton Island in Greenland, about 260 miles south. The men were to sledge north through a part of Ellesmere Island called Grinnell Land, after a New York shipowner who had paid for two expeditions to find Franklin, and meet Greely, who had been ordered to abandon his camp no later than September of 1883 if no one had reached him. Greely was to travel by boat along the coast of Grinnell Land in the hope of meeting the sledgers or else of making it to Littleton Island.

Greely was thirty-eight when he left for the Arctic. He was born in Massachusetts in 1844. His father was a shoemaker. Greely was not an especially good student, and in 1861 he enlisted in the Massachusetts Volunteer Infantry. He was at the Battle of Yorktown, and was wounded twice at Antietam, the most fatal battle of the Civil War, where 23,000 men died in twelve hours. After he recovered he was made second lieutenant in the Ninth Regiment, Corps d'Afrique, which was stationed in Louisiana. To try to recover wages owed to his troops, he wrote to his superiors in Washington that "colored soldiers deserve as much as white soldiers, as they are fighting for the same cause." After the war the army sent him west, and by 1873 he was a member of the Signal Corps, the branch that supports the troops with information, and was mostly involved in sending weather bulletins to Washington. The following year he went to Texas to string telegraph lines through bandit and Indian territory.

Greely was tall and wiry and wore glasses, and he had never been to the Arctic but had read a lot about it. As close as he had come was to live through a three-day blizzard on the plains. He liked discipline, he didn't like gambling, and he forbade his men to curse—he appeared, in other words, to be something of a prig. Three years before leaving, he had gotten married, and he and his wife had two children. When he left the *Proteus,* he wrote her, "I think of you always and most continually. I wonder what you and the darling babes are doing. I desire continually you and your society, our home and its comforts. I am content at being here only that I hope from and through it the future may be made brighter and happier for you and the children. Will it? We will so hope and trust. There seems so little outside of you and the babes that is of any real and true value to me."

Motley parties of servicemen and civilians didn't usually do well in the Arctic. The servicemen were accustomed to hierarchical discipline, and the citizens were not accustomed to discipline at all. Greely's crew had nineteen soldiers, three who had been mustered into service for the purpose, two Greenland natives as hunters and guides, and a civilian doctor, Octave Pavy, who was also the expedition's naturalist and the last person to join. Pavy had been born in 1844 in New Orleans, but he was sent to France as a child to be educated. He had come back to America in 1872 to undertake "The Pavy Expedition to the North Pole," but his backer died before he could leave. In 1879, he joined another Arctic expedition, which was given up in Greenland when its ship was judged unfit. The ship went home, but Pavy stayed, learning to speak Eskimo and, according to his wife, Lilla May Pavy, making "himself an adept, so far as a foreigner can become such, in the management of the Eskimo sledge." (Lilla May Pavy was from St. Louis, but another woman turned up from Paris and said she was also married to Pavy.) In addition, he collected plants, rocks, and animals he stuffed, and studied diseases specific to the region and how to treat them. He was a little prickly and regarded himself as better educated and more knowledgeable about the Arctic than Greely and the others. Greely had command of him, since Pavy was, nominally, for the expedition, a soldier, but he pretty much refused to be bossed or only acceded resentfully.

The *Proteus* left them at the northern end of Ellesmere Island, across from Greenland, about eleven hundred miles above the Arctic Circle, then got caught in the ice before it could leave. On flat ground about a hundred yards from the shore, they built Fort Conger. Perhaps two hundred yards from it they also built a small hut as a place to make magnetic observations.

Before a month had passed Greely had reprimanded his two lieutenants, Lockwood and Kislingbury, for sleeping late. Lockwood, an insomniac, reformed, but not Kislingbury. Kislingbury had strung telegraph lines with Greely in Texas, and Greely had invited him. Three years earlier Kislingbury's wife had died, and he had married her sister and then she died, too, apparently of scarlet fever at Fort Custer while Kislingbury had been gone several weeks on a scouting mission. By his two wives he had four sons, two of whom also came down with scarlet fever but recovered. He wrote Greely that the expedition would be an opportunity "to wear out my second terrible sorrow." His sons, he wrote, "will love me better when I return and will be proud of the father who dared to brave the dangers we have read about of a sojourn in the Arctic regions," then added, "You will find no truer friend or devoted servant."

For three days, with the *Proteus* still in view, Greely held breakfast half an hour for Kislingbury. When reproached, Kislingbury said they should have started without him. Officers should not have to rise with the enlisted men anyway, he added. Greely said that the agreeable compliance with orders was essential to an officer's usefulness. Kislingbury said nothing and walked away. He wrote Greely a letter saying morosely that he felt that Greely had no confidence in him, and might prefer that he left.

Greely called the officers to a conference far enough away from the hut that the men couldn't hear him, and read the letter to Pavy, Lockwood, and Kislingbury. Then he said that he didn't go in for intimations and if he wanted an officer removed, he would say so. Kislingbury, perhaps from hurt feelings, said that the effect of Greely's treatment had amounted to as much. Greely asked Kislingbury if he still wished to be relieved, and Kislingbury said yes.

Carrying his bags, Kislingbury was walking toward the *Proteus,* half a mile away, when a passage opened in the ice and the ship sailed off. Disbelieving, he watched it for some time. Then he walked back to Fort Conger. Greely wrote orders specifying that Kislingbury was to be treated as someone "temporarily at this station awaiting transportation"—as a citizen, in other words, someone unable to ask a soldier to do the simplest thing for him.

The *Proteus's* leaving signified the start of their term. With the ship, Greely wrote, went "my intense longing to get back to my wife and children." He announced that on the Sabbath no games could be played, and that even those among the crew who were not religious would have to listen to him read from Psalms. The first one he chose was 133, which begins, "Behold, how good and how pleasant it is for brethren to dwell together in unity."

In October, Greely climbed a hill to watch the sun disappear. During the Arctic night the North Star seemed to hang overhead like a distant lantern. The Great Bear and Orion's Belt were the brightest constellations. The dark was so thick at times that they couldn't read a wristwatch, and on occasion they saw the moon for days at a time.

Commander Winfield Schley, the officer who eventually rescued them, wrote in his report, "Over everything was dead silence, so horribly oppressive that a man alone is almost tempted to kill himself, so lonely does he feel."

They hunted musk ox and drew coal from a mine that was three miles away. Despite their intimate terms, they knew only so much about one another. Sergeant David Ralston's birthday they celebrated with a meal of oyster soup, roast beef, vegetables, jelly cake, peach pie, cherry pie, and coffee, unaware that Ralston's wife had been a widow who said that Ralston had married her for her late husband's money, and had left her destitute. Dr. Pavy embarked on a sledge trip to establish depots for other sledge trips and returned early, going only half as far as he had been expected to, but had been stopped by ice, he said, which annoyed Greely, who thought Pavy at least ought to have waited for the tide to turn to see if the ice moved.

In the darkness resentments accumulated between Greely and Pavy, but sometimes also with and among the men. Greely announced that the soldiers would have to do the officers' laundry, asked for volunteers, and got none. He told a sergeant named David Brainard to assign someone. When the men's response was to feel aggrieved, Greely, according to Brainard's journal, said that "he was not a man to be trifled with and in case of mutiny he would not stop at the loss of human lives to restore order."

To invoke routines from regular life, they ate with silver-plated knives and forks on linen that they changed twice a week. Each day they made five hundred notations from their instruments, including a pendulum. They made observations of the northern lights, which Greely described as resembling "a beautiful and brilliant arch formed of convoluted bends of lights similar to twisted ribbons," and another time as "lances of white light, perhaps tinged with gold or citrine." To keep the men outdoors for an hour a day, Greely had Brainard invent projects. Around the hut, for example, three feet from the walls, they built a barrier of ice six feet tall, so that falling snow would fill in the interval and insulate the place. They spread gravel and sand on the floor to

make it smooth enough to sleep on. Against boredom Greely began teaching math, grammar, geography, and the weather science he had learned in the Signal Corps. He also spoke twice a month about other polar expeditions and the Civil War. Lieutenant Lockwood edited "Arctic Moon," a broadsheet with news and commentary contributed by "the finest minds of the country." They established depots and mapped parts of the interior. Their triumph was Lieutenant Lockwood's traveling nearly a thousand miles by sledge, reaching eighty-three degrees twenty-five minutes north, by four miles the farthest north ever—about halfway to the pole, and three hundred miles north of Fort Conger. "Before them all was new," the naval report said of Lockwood and the men in his party. They had traveled in territory "which had never before met the vision of civilized man."

The first member to crack in the prevalent darkness was Jens Edward, one of the Greenlanders, who wandered from camp and was brought back by men who followed his tracks for ten miles. Not long after Edward's collapse, the other Greenlander, Thorlip Frederick Christiansen, who was called Eskimo Fred, began waving a cross at the others, whom he believed meant to shoot him. He was eventually pacified. Greely and Pavy indulged their dislike of each other. Pavy wrote in his journal that Greely was full of vanity, and Greely wrote that Pavy was tricky and two-faced, "idle, unfit for any Arctic work except doctoring and sledge travel and not first class in the latter."

The ship that was to relieve them, the *Neptune,* got no closer to Fort Conger than 150 miles when its captain tried to force the ship through a lead and its boiler burst. At Littleton Island and at Cape Sabine, three hundred miles south, he left small caches of food, each sufficient for ten days. He also left a whaleboat at each place. His orders were to return with his provisions if he hadn't reached Fort Conger. He tried once more to advance, and went home with enough food to sustain a retreat lasting two and a half months, should Greely find it necessary to abandon Fort Conger to reach the next summer's ship.

17

No one got along any better during the second winter. "Perfect ease of mind cannot come until a ship is seen again," Greely wrote in the spring. He prepared for the ship's arrival by, among other tasks, ordering that a catalog be made of all the natural-history specimens collected. Dr. Pavy's military commission ended on July 20. On the nineteenth Greely asked for his records and his diary. Pavy gave up the records but not the diary, saying that it was a private account and had no place in the expedition's archive. Greely had him arrested.

The second relief ship was the *Proteus,* which had brought them to the Arctic. It was accompanied by the *Yantic.* The *Proteus* sailed farther than the *Neptune* but got caught in the ice and sank slowly. While it was going down, the captain ordered that the ship's supplies be thrown onto the ice, but most of the crew gave up their posts to save their belongings. About a third of what went overboard went into the water. What remained was left at Cape Sabine for Greely. Then the crew rowed lifeboats south to the *Yantic.*

A man named Henry Clay, who was initially a member of the expedition but had quarreled with Dr. Pavy and quit only days before it left, wrote a letter to the *Louisville Courier-Journal* saying that if a ship did not reach Fort Conger by September, Greely would have to leave for Cape Sabine, more than 250 miles away. If he made 5 miles a day, Clay wrote, it would take him until November to arrive, and by then night would have fallen for the winter. "Their condition will be truly pitiable," Clay wrote. Likely they would be stranded at Cape Sabine, where they would run out of food. Then they would "lie down on the cold ground, under the quiet stars," being "past all earthly succor."

In August of 1883, enacting the plan to retreat if no one had come for them after two years, and leaving dishes on the table and the beds unmade, collections of lichens and moss and fossils, ten musical instruments, some stuffed birds and some sealskin coats, twenty-three dogs, with enough food to last in case the expedition returned, and nailing the door shut, Greely and his men left Fort Conger in their steam launch, which was named *Lady Greely.* The launch towed two smaller boats and a dinghy, which were loaded with their diaries and records, their scientific instruments, including chronometers and the pendulum, four rifles, two shotguns, a thousand rounds, and Greely's dress uniform with his sword. Sergeant William Cross described the flotilla as resembling a "load of trash." They had occupied Fort Conger for 721 days, 268 of them in darkness. The dogs barked as the expedition departed.

18

For thirteen days they drifted among pack ice, "suffering horribly from the cold," according to the naval report. When a lead opened, they had to wonder if it would stay open or close while they were in it and wreck them. Waves broke over them sometimes, and it snowed. The officers' journals are full of bickering about Greely's decisions. He wanted to abandon the boats and drift on the ice. While he slept, Pavy told Brainard and Rice that if Greely insisted, Pavy would pronounce him unstable and replace him. Greely's "frequent outbursts of passion evinced insanity," Pavy said. Under Kislingbury—whose position, if he hadn't lost it, would have made him second in command—they would return to Fort Conger and try to leave again in the spring. Brainard realized that he was required to report the exchange to Greely, but he was concerned that if he did, Greely would act in such a way as to deliver himself into Pavy's hands. Brainard was as close to an ally as Greely had, but he wrote, "All that ignorance, stupidity, and an egotistical mind without judgment can do in the injury of our cause is being done."

Pavy's plan became unnecessary when Greely called the officers to a meeting in the launch. He told them that the circumstances being what they were, he had no right to act alone. "I am not infallible," he said.

To try to reach land, they left the launch and crossed the ice.

A few times they came within two or three miles of shore, but a gale moved the ice and carried them off. In August, on a flyspeck piece of rock called Washington Irving Island, they found food left in 1875 by the British polar expedition led by George Nares. The cache was small and mostly rotten. Among it were tins of dog biscuits, which they opened. In all there were 110 pounds of biscuits, only 58 of which were preserved. The rest were "a mass of filthy green mould." Greely ordered the spoiled ones thrown away, but the men found them and ate them until Greely forbade them to. A few days later, Lockwood wrote, "Occupied some time this morning in scraping, like a dog, in the place where the moulded dog-biscuits were emptied. Found a few crumbs of small pieces, and ate mould and all."

In the third week of September the worst storm they had seen sent waves washing over their floe, "the spray freezing to them and causing them intense suffering," the report said. They waited for the waves to break up the floe and drown them. Instead another floe drifted close to theirs, and they climbed onto it and from there on September 29, after 51 days at sea, they arrived at Eskimo Point, about twenty miles south of Cape Sabine. While the party collected stones for a shelter, Sergeant Rice and Jens Edward walked to Cape Sabine, hoping to find either a ship or food one had left. In a cairn, they found a note telling them that the *Proteus* had sunk. It also told them where to find three small caches of food which were sufficient for less than a month. The report they brought Greely "sent a thrill of horror to every heart," the naval officer wrote. "Every one knew that death must come to nearly all of the party long before the ship of rescue could force its way."

Greely decided to move to Cape Sabine. "It is not easy to give an idea of the desolate and horrible aspect of this bleak and barren spot," Schley wrote when they reached it. "To the north is the sea, filled with ice," and behind it were glaciers and mountains. All around was "barren rock, except where the snow still lay deep in the hollows." From stones, they built a shelter twenty-five feet long and seventeen wide, which hardly held them all. The walls were four feet tall and three feet thick and were chinked with loose rocks and moss. To make a lodgepole, they stood their whaleboat on end and over it they stretched a canvas sail. Snow fell and covered it. They named their refuge Camp Clay, after Henry Clay.

Among the food from the *Proteus* were some lemons wrapped in newspapers. From the newspapers the men learned that Chester Arthur had become president after Garfield had been shot. The papers, astonishingly, included Henry Clay's letter, which also said, "The cache of 240 rations, if it can be found, will prolong their misery for a few days."

Within weeks everyone was desperately hungry. Some of the food had rotted and was buried, but a few of the soldiers dug it up and ate it anyway. Hoping to make what they had last the winter, Greely allowed each man fifteen ounces of food a day. These included six and a half ounces of bread and dog biscuits; four and a half ounces of meat and blubber; one and two-fifths ounces of canned vegetables and rice; one ounce of berries, pickles, raisins and milk; nine-tenths of an ounce of soup and beef-extract; and three-quarters of an ounce of butter and lard.

In early November, Greely sent four soldiers—George Rice, Julius Frederick, Joseph Elison, and David Linn—to retrieve 144 pounds of meat he thought had been left forty miles away by the Nares expedition. Eight days later Rice returned at two in the morning, exhausted, and said, "Elison is dying at Ross Bay."

Thirst is a constant threat in the Arctic, and Elison had gotten so thirsty that he had eaten snow, which should never be done. To begin with, it is painful. According to Julius von Payer, an Austro-Hungarian explorer from what is now the Czech Republic, colder than thirty-seven degrees below zero, snow feels in the mouth, "like a hot iron." It is also impossible to eat a sufficient amount to slake one's thirst. Furthermore, eating snow was seen as a failure of character. "Snow-eaters during the march were regarded by us as weaklings much in the same way as opium-eaters are," Payer wrote.

The snow froze Elison's hands and face. The others tried to warm his hands by placing them between their thighs. "The poor fellow cried all night from the pain," Frederick wrote. In addition, his feet has frozen and he couldn't stand. To carry him on the sledge they had to leave the meat behind. The next night they had to warm him again. The following day his face became frosted, and his eyelids froze shut. A gale arrived. Linn and Frederick got into the sleeping bag on either side of Elison, and Rice started for the camp, which was twenty-five miles away. To walk there took sixteen hours. In the meantime Frederick and Linn lay in the sleeping bag with Elison, whose lips were frozen together, so he couldn't take any of the beef they tried to feed him. He merely lay groaning. His suffering was so difficult for Linn to bear that he tried to leave the bag, which would have meant dying from exposure, and Frederick had to hold him back. Elison wet himself and his urine soaked the bag and froze, so for eighteen hours they lay as if clamped in place.

When the rescuers reached them, Elison said, "Please kill me, will you?" To get him out of the bag, they had to cut it apart. They wrapped him in a blanket and placed him on a sledge. His feet had turned black.

Greely could think of no other way to divert the men's attention from their suffering, so he began lecturing again, about geography and the states. "Talked for nearly two hours to-day on the State of Maine," he wrote, "touching on its climate, its vegetable and mineral products, its river system, mountain ranges, principal cities, its most important resources and manufactures, its history and the famous men who have come from the State;

and also as to its inducements to emigrants to settle within its limits. Subsequently I called upon Jewell, who has lived in Maine, to supplement my statements by any additional information he might possess; and, late, invited questions from any of the party on mooted or neglected points." Private Henry, because he had the most penetrating voice, read aloud. On November 24, "Instead of the customary reading from the Bible, Dickens, and the Army Regulations," Greely wrote, "this evening was given up to reminiscences pertaining to the past lives and domestic surroundings of the men."

Food began to disappear. "During last night someone, without doubt, took bread from Corporal Elison's bread-can," Greely wrote on December 4. "I was awake, and plainly heard it done." A knife used to open a milk tin stolen from the storehouse belonged to a soldier named Schneider, who said he had lent the knife to Pvt. Charles B. Henry. Henry's real name was Charles Henry Buck, but they didn't know it. (A thief and a forger, he had also killed a man in a fight and gone to prison for it. After being kicked out of the cavalry, he had signed up with his new name.)

Game was scarce, and neither Greenlander had any luck hunting. By the middle of November, Greely lowered rations to four ounces a day. "We are all more or less unreasonable," Brainard wrote in his journal, "and I can only wonder that we are not all insane."

Lockwood made lists of meals he planned to eat after being rescued. In the middle of other notations, he would sometimes insert references to food. "Oranges and pineapples cut up together, and eaten with grated cocoanut," one of them says; then he went on to wonder whether his father was alive and if he would see him again. On another occasion he wrote, "Brainard is to come to supper at my home on reaching Washington, and I have promised him sally lun, stewed oysters, smearkase, and preserved strawberries with cake. After supper a smoke, and then wine and cake." Also, "I have invited Fredericks and Long to come to the house and eat some preserved strawberries and black cake."

Cross died first. He had been splitting wood, then he fell into a coma and died two days later. Pavy thought scurvy had killed him. According to the naval report, however, he died "from the use of liquor. He would drink anything that had a suspicion of alcohol about it, even paint." They sewed him up in canvas sacks, Greely read the burial service over him, then they hauled him on a sledge to a hill above a lake, which Greely named Cross Lake. "A ghostly procession of emaciated men moving slowly and silently away from their wretched ice prison in the uncertain light," is how Brainard described them. Not having the tools they needed, they dug a grave with their hands and placed on it a ring of stones. Cross died the day before he would have been forty. They discovered that he had saved up bread and butter to celebrate.

In his excellent *Ghosts of Cape Sabine,* Leonard Guttridge describes their routines in the days following the funeral. "The men kept mostly to their sleeping bags. Those who managed to leave the hut did so only from physical necessity. Few read. Frost and ice coated the interior walls. In the dim blubber-fueled lamplight, the commander strained weak eyes over psalms and poetry, his voice barely audible above buffeting wind gusts. Lieutenant Lockwood improvised a lecture on the St. Louis riots, and while smoking a blend of tobacco and tea leaves, he dreamed of a restaurant in that city named The Silver Moon, where fifty cents bought a dinner, and a nearby bakery offered 'excellent bread and something fine in the way of tapioca and coconut pies.' The lieutenant interrupted his soliloquy to hand Sergeant Ralston a piece of tobacco for plugging a painfully hollow tooth.

This makeshift filling enabled Ralston to murmur memories of early days as an Iowa farmhand. Then he read from *The Pickwick Papers*. Brainard talked of Indian fighting; Pavy described a bull-fight and a walking tour through Switzerland. Such efforts were to sustain morale." Greely one day asked the men to help him make a "chronological table of all the principal events of the world."

They engaged in what Lockwood described as "several wordy disputes," one involving "the differences between coons, opos-sums, etc.," and they followed bird tracks in the snow, hoping to shoot the bird.

Elison's frostbitten fingers dropped off. Dr. Pavy cut through the small piece of skin at the ankle that held his foot. His other foot fell off two days later on its own.

Lockwood was unable one day to rise from his sleeping bag, and was raving. "He can understand many things only after sev-eral repetitions," Greely wrote. Lockwood had secretly saved his bread until he had a pound and a half, and then he had eaten it all and got sick. Private Whisler began challenging people to step outside and fight, and one day he fought in his sleeping bag with Private Bender, whom he shared the bag with.

In March the sun returned, and Christiansen and Francis Long, looking for game, traveled seventy-five miles without crossing a track. Greely described the party as "twenty-four starved men, of whom two cannot walk and a half dozen cannot haul a pound." Lockwood wrote, "The time draws near when our group comes to an end. We look on it with equanimity, and the spirits of the party, with this prospect of a miserable death, are certainly wonderful. I am glad as each day draws to an end. It puts us nearer the end of this life—whatever that end is to be." Greely added, "It drives me almost insane to face the future. It is not the end that afrights any one but the road to be travelled to reach that goal. To die is easy." What was difficult was "to strive, to endure, to live." It was "easier to think of death than to dare to live."

At the foot of a glacier about a mile from the camp was a tidal pool where Rice began setting nets for shrimps, using skins as bait, and sometimes seaweed until he grew too tired to collect it. The shrimp were almost entirely shell and very small—they were called sea flies, and eight hundred of them weighed an ounce. No one liked them, but they ate them.

In March the Eskimo hunter Jens Edward said that he saw Private Henry steal bacon and hide it under his shirt. That night Henry threw up the bacon. At a meeting in the morning, others said that they had also known Henry to steal food. "A clamor for his life was raised, but repressed by me," Greely wrote. Instead Henry was confined to his sleeping bag "except under the supervision of his comrades." Two days later ten ounces of chocolate that had been saved for Elison were missing, and Henry was suspected, but no one could say anything definitely.

Later Henry was discovered drunk on liquor stolen from the tiny store of rum on hand. "A second time his life was demanded, but again I spared him," Greely wrote. He reminded Henry that unity was essential. Then, not trusting him, he wrote out an order that if Henry were caught stealing again, he was to be shot.

At the beginning of April, the Eskimo, Fred Christiansen, began talking nonsense, and the next day he died. David Linn died the following day, pleading for water, of which there was none. Both were buried shallowly on the hill.

Even though Sergeant Rice was not well, he and Julius Frederick volunteered to collect the beef that had been abandoned in the fall when Elison had been frozen. They had been asking to go for some time, but Greely had not let them, "foreseeing the great chances of a fatal result." Having finally persuaded Greely that the errand was necessary, they asked that they not be given any extra rations so that no one would suffer any deprivation if they didn't return. To rest before leaving, Rice shared a sleeping bag with Linn, who was dead. His own bag had been loaded on the sledge.

They left at midnight on April 6. While they were away, Lockwood died early one morning, and—concerned that he might die himself—Greely restored Kislingbury to his rank, meaning, he said, that "in the event of my death the command of the expedition will devolve on you."

Half miraculously, the men killed a bear that came near the camp. Meanwhile Jewell lapsed into a delirium and died. The bear froze and had to be dressed with a handsaw, which hardly anyone had the strength for. One of the men noticed that Greely's hands trembled, as if from a palsy, and he wrote, "I hardly think he knows how weak he is."

"Our condition grows more horrible every day," Greely wrote. "No man knows when death is coming, and each has long since faced it unmoved. Each man who has died has passed into the preliminary stages of mental, but never violent, wandering without a suspicion that death has marked him. Only those who lived knew, and at the first wanderings we looked at each other, conscious that still another was about to pass away."

After three days Frederick and Rice reached the place where they thought they had left the cache, but they couldn't find the rifle they had stood in the snow to mark it. They concluded that the ice had drifted and taken it. To search for the cache, they had left their sledge. Walking back to it, Rice's feet froze, and then he became too weak to go farther. Frederick gave him spirits of ammonia in rum, and they walked half a mile to the sledge, and in the lee of an iceberg collapsed. Rice talked about his family and friends, his home, and the things he planned to eat when he got there. Frederick took off his jacket to try to warm Rice's feet;

then, on a "desolate piece of ice with the wind blowing a hurricane," he held him until he died, which took a few hours. What Frederick wished he could do was lie down and die beside Rice, but he knew Greely would send others to look for him, who might die in the effort. He kissed Rice, then walked seven miles to their camp where they had left the sleeping bag, which was "frozen stiff as cordwood." After sniffing a vial of ammonia he was able to force the bag open. In the morning he walked back to bury Rice. "I had no shovel, only an axe, and the loose ice I had to remove with my hands," he wrote.

The death of his friend "made a deeper impression on my mind than any experience in my whole life," Frederick wrote in a report. He walked for three days to reach Camp Clay and when he arrived he gave Greely the food that Rice hadn't eaten.

At the end of April, ice tore a hole in Jens Edward's kayak while he was stalking a seal, and he drowned. Without the kayak they couldn't hunt seals. Furthermore, Edward had gone under with their best rifle, a Springfield. "We are in the most abject misery," Private Roderick Schneider wrote, "and those that are dead are surely the best off."

Brainard still walked to the shrimp ground, passing the graves on the hill. According to the navy report, after the last stored food was given out in the middle of May, "the party subsisted on lichens, moss, saxifrage, sealskin, both boiled and roasted, and a little tea." Greely wrote to his wife, "The whole party are prepared to die and I feel certain that they will face death quietly and decently."

Pavy asked Greely to write a letter attesting that he had conducted himself as he should have. He wanted it for his wife, he said. Greely wrote it reluctantly, and gave copies to Brainard and Israel, because he feared that Pavy would alter it. Except for Pavy's medical service, his record "has been mighty bad," Greely wrote in his journal. "I say all this on the edge of the grave."

William Ellis, perhaps deranged, drew up a will leaving his pay to his mother and his son, although his son had died before the expedition had left, and then he died, apparently starved. Then Ralson, then Whisler, then Israel, whom Greely was especially fond of "died at 2 a.m., very hard," Schneider wrote. "He struggled long for life." Fourteen were left, and the bulk of them decided to abandon their hut because water from melting snow kept dripping into it so that "we are saturated to the skin and are in a wretched condition," Greely wrote. Eleven of them moved a few hundred feet up the hill to a tent. Some were able to walk on their own, but others needed to be carried. The tent was crowded. One night Brainard had to sleep outside in a storm because the two men he shared his sleeping bag with, one of them Pavy, wouldn't make room for him. Corporal Nicholas Salor died next, and no one had the strength to carry him up the hill and bury him. He was "put out of sight on the icefoot," meaning where the ice met the shore. Pavy appeared to be the strongest man left. He would go to a ridge behind the tent and chop ice to melt for water, for which Greely was grateful.

19

On the first of June, Kislingbury sat up in his sleeping bag in the middle of a gale, and began singing a hymn. He died a few hours later. His body was taken out into the snow and the service said over him, but he was left where he lay. "Party will try to bury him tomorrow," Greely wrote.

The bay was now free of ice. "How easily we could be rescued," Greely noted. Pavy prescribed medicine for Maurice

Connell and for Bender, but Greely "forbade the issue," Schneider wrote, "saying that the doctor was not in a way to order medicine."

Private Henry was suspected again of stealing food. He promised Greely he would stop, but Greely didn't believe him. His order to his three sergeants said that in light of the party's "perishing slowly by starvation," it was essential that if Henry were "detected either eating food or appropriating any article of provisions," he be shot. "Any other course would be a fatal leniency, the man being able to overcome any two of our present force."

The next morning Henry "not only stole shrimps for our breakfast, but visiting unauthorized our winter camp, stole certain sealskins for food." Greely confronted Henry as he returned from the hut, and Henry admitted the theft. "He was bold in his admission, and showed neither fear nor contrition," Greely noted. In his tent, he wrote,

Near Cape Sabine, June 4, 1884
Sergeants Brainard, Long and Frederick

Notwithstanding promises given by Private C. B. Henry yesterday, he has since, as acknowledged to me, tampered with seal-thongs, if not other food at the old camp. This pertinacity and audacity is the destruction of the party, if not at once ended. Private Henry will be shot to-day, all care being taken to prevent his injuring anyone, as his physical strength is greater than that of any two men. Decide the manner of his death by two ball and one blank cartridge. This order is IMPERATIVE and ABSOLUTELY NECESSARY for ANY CHANCE of life.

The sergeants were not sure how to perform the task—whether it was proper to tell Henry and allow him time to settle himself, or if they should simply shoot him without warning. Early in the afternoon they went down the hill to the hut. About half an hour later Frederick came back and told Henry he was needed, and Henry went down the hill with him. The others heard three shots. Months later Frederick described what had happened: "He did not know that we were about to kill him, but he had been warned," Frederick said. "We walked to within twenty yards of him" to read him Greely's order. "There was no missing him at that range," Frederick said. "Without a word the man dropped dead." They agreed not to disclose whose bullet had killed him. Hidden among his belongings were twelve pounds of sealskin.

A few hours later Private Bender, who had also stolen food, died "very cowardly for a man who has said so much about meeting death," Schneider wrote, then Dr. Pavy, who drank extract of ergot from the medicine chest, possibly thinking it was iron and that he was fortifying himself. When sealskin was found among Pavy's belongings, too, Schneider felt vindicated, since he had also been accused of stealing. His remarks form one of the most haunting declarations in the history of Arctic service. "Although I am a dying man, I deny the assertion," he wrote. "I ate only my own boots and part of an old pair of pants I received from Lieutenant Kislingbury." Then he added, "I feel myself going fast, but I wish it would go yet faster."

Seven men were left. "Every one of us much used up," Schneider wrote. Strangely the strongest appeared to be Elison, who had lost his feet and hands but had been given extra food. Biederbeck, who looked after him closely, had fashioned a spoon to fit one of his stumps.

Brainard continued to walk to the bay for shrimp, but on the tenth of June he wrote that his nets were lost and his bait gone also. On the twelfth he walked to the top of a hill about a hundred feet above the water and put up a flag made from rags, hoping that a whaler might see it. The wind blew it down, and the next day he climbed the hill again to put it back up.

Sitting in his sleeping bag, a soldier named Hampdon Gardiner held a portrait of his mother and another of his wife, whom he had married only two months before he had boarded the *Proteus*. While talking to them, he died. Two days later he was left on the ice foot, where Pavy and Bender had also been left. The wind had partly uncovered the corpses on the hill, enough so that the buttons on their clothes could be seen. On the seventeenth Schneider wrote, "I am unable to use my legs," and on the eighteenth, begging for opium, he died. The others managed to get him halfway to the ice foot but could go no farther and left him.

Remembering that it was approximately "the average date of whalers reaching the north water," Greely said, they began to look for ships. He stayed mostly in his sleeping bag and lapsed in and out of consciousness. Early in the third week of June, a gale blew down the tent, and no one had the strength to put it back up. They lay as if under a shroud.

On the twentieth Greely wrote, "Six years ago to-day I was married and three years ago I left my wife for this Expedition, what contrast! When will this life in death end?"

Just before midnight on June 21, 1884, through a gale, Greely heard a whistling sound, which no one else heard, and when he asked Brainard and Long if they could manage to see what it was, "they thought it only the impression of a disturbed imagination," Schley wrote in "The Rescue of Greely," published in 1885. Brainard returned without Long and said the noise had been made by the wind. He got back into his sleeping bag.

One of Schley's crew, on an island called Brevoort Island, not far from Camp Clay, had found a cairn that Greely had built in the fall. In it were papers that he brought back to the ship. To recall the rest of the searchers, Schley had the ship's whistle blown, and this is the sound Greely heard. The papers, which were read aloud, described the expedition's stay at Fort Conger and the retreat. "As one paper after another was quickly turned over," Schley wrote, "it was discovered with horror that the latest date borne by any of them was October 21, 1883, and that but forty days' complete rations were left to live upon. Eight months had lapsed since then."

In the next-to-last entry, for October 6, Greely had written, "My party is now permanently encamped on the 'west side of a small neck of land,'" which he went on to say was "about equally distant from Cape Sabine and Cocked Hat Island. All well."

With the wind "driving in bitter gusts," Schley wrote, the mission's navigator, Lieutenant Colwell, piloted their steam cutter into the cove off Cape Sabine. It was eight o'clock on a Sunday night, broad daylight but overcast—"the daylight of a dull winter afternoon," Schley wrote. Rounding a point, the men saw a figure at the top of a low hill. They waved a flag at him, and Long bent over and picked up a flag and waved it. Then he walked slowly and carefully toward the boat, falling down twice before reaching the shore. "He was a ghastly sight," Schley wrote. "His cheeks were hollow, his eyes wild, his hair and beard long and matted. His army blouse, covering several thicknesses of shirts and jackets, was ragged and dirty. He wore a little fur cap and rough moccasins of untanned leather tied around the leg. As he spoke, his utterances were thick and mumbling, and in his agitation his jaws worked in convulsive twitches."

Lieutenant Colwell led a party up the hill, arriving at the tent just as Brainard was stepping from it. Brainard was about to salute, but Colwell reached for his hand. "Meanwhile one of the relief party, who in his agitation and excitement was crying like a child, was down on his hands and knees trying to roll away the stones that held down the flapping tent cloth," Schley wrote. With a knife Colwell slit the tent cover. What he saw "was a sight of horror. On one side, close to the opening, with his head towards the outside, lay what was apparently a dead man. His jaw had dropped, his eyes were open, but fixed and glassy, his limbs were motionless." This was Connell, who was, however, still alive. "On the opposite side was a poor fellow, alive to be sure, but without hands or feet, and with a spoon tied to the stump of his right arm." Two men were trying to pour something from a bottle into a can—"the pitiful ration of tanned oil, sealskin, and lichens that they called their meal," the navy report says, but Schley says it was brandy, the last few teaspoons left, which they were giving to Connell, "of whom all hope had been given up." A third, also on "hands and knees, was a dark man with a long, matted beard, in a dirty and tattered dressing gown. The man wore "a little red skull cap" above "brilliant, staring eyes." He raised himself slightly and put on wire-framed glasses. Colwell asked, "Who are you?" The man only stared at him. When Colwell asked again, one of the others said, "That's the Major—Major Greely." Colwell crawled into the tent and took his hand. He said, "Greely, is this you?"

Greely said, "Yes. Seven of us left. Here we are, dying like men. Did what we came to do. Beat the best record." Then he collapsed.

Colwell gave them some biscuits and shavings of pemmican, a substance made from dried meat, fat, and berries. Since they couldn't stand, they knelt, and held out their hands. After each had had two servings, Colwell told them that they had eaten all they could safely ingest, "but their hunger had come back full force and they begged piteously." Their hunger returned, Schley wrote, "like a drunkard's craving for rum." When Greely was refused more, he produced a can of "boiled sealksin, which had been carefully husbanded, and which he said he had a right to eat, as it was his own." Colwell threw away the pemmican can, but while he was trying to raise the tent, one of the men found it and scraped from it what was left.

Colwell built a small fire and every ten minutes for two hours fed them milk punch and beef extract while he waited for the doctor to arrive and tell him it was safe to move them. Except for Greely, none of them seemed especially affected by their rescue. "The weaker ones were like children," Schley wrote, "petulant, rambling and fitful in their talk, absent and sometimes a little incoherent." To cheer them Colwell told them that more people were coming and that relief was at hand, but they "could not realize it and refused to believe it." Schley went on to speculate that "their year of privation and hopelessness had blunted or deadened their recollection of the world, as they had known it, and the feelings to which the recollections gave rise."

Schley had two ships and the men were carried to them on stretchers. Frederick said that he was strong enough to walk, but a man had to stand on either side of him. "Leaning on their shoulders, he followed the slow procession as it wound its way around the rocks and through the snow-fill hollows to the sea," Schley wrote.

The gale had become a hurricane. Crossing the hundred yards to the ships, Greely and the others got "a severe wetting." Having been taken below, Greely fainted but was revived with spirits of ammonia.

When Brainard was undressed, calluses more than half an inch thick were found on his knees. "After so many months in the desolate Arctic regions, after so much suffering, and passing through such scenes of horror, it was seldom that the men stood upright," the report says. "They crawled about on their hands and knees over the rock and ice."

20

Once the men were aboard, the party retrieved the dead men from graves out of which some of their hands and feet protruded. The five men who had been left on the ice foot had disappeared, apparently taken by the tide. The officers who dug up the corpses called for blankets and rolled up the bodies without letting anyone see them. In the hurricane they were loaded aboard the ships, which had difficulty staying head to the wind. Two of the bodies went into the water, but were "recovered by one of the seamen before they could sink," Schley wrote. Still wrapped in blankets, they were put into coffins and then the lids were riveted into place.

Some of the sailors who had handled the remains thought that they seemed very light, and that some of the blankets seemed to contain only half a body. "Giving the allowance for the imagination of the sailors," the naval report said, "the hard facts of the few who saw the remains and related what they saw to others before silence was enjoined show that terrible scenes must have been enacted by the famishing men in the Greely camp during the many long months that famine was with them."

On the way home they stopped at Disko to bury the Greenlander, Fred Christiansen, Eskimo Fred. In the pastor's remarks one can hear the cadence of the nineteenth century. "No man knows the thought of God concerning us," he said. "He whose soulless body we are today to bury, and the other, his companion, who perished in a kayak in the northern regions, did not think their days were numbered when they took leave of the wives they loved and of the children who were to be their support in old age."

Two days passed before Greely could sit up in bed for a few hours, and for his hunger to begin to leave him. Elison, who had lost his fingers and feet, died aboard his ship when his wounds turned septic. Apparently in the cold the bacteria they contained had been dormant. "He passed away quietly without apparent suffering," Schley wrote.

The navy ordered Schley's crew not to speak to anyone about the rescue, but someone must have. In August the *New York Times* printed a story with the headline, "Horrors of Cape Sabine," saying that some of the bodies had been clumsily mutilated and the others skillfully. The skillful ones had been done apparently by Dr. Pavy. When he died, the other cuts were made. Pavy and the men who died after him were the ones who had washed away, and the circumstance was seen as being meant to conceal the cannibalism. Lieutenant Kislingbury's three brothers were persuaded by a newspaper in Rochester, New York, to have his remains examined, and they discovered that flesh had been cut from him. Then Private William Whisler's parents, who lived in Indiana, had his body examined. What was left of him was hardly more than a skeleton.

Greely said he had been unaware of what the others had been doing. "I can give no stronger denial," he wrote, but he said that he could not answer for anyone else. *Three Years of Arctic Service* was published in 1886. He retired from the army in 1907 as a major general and was the first president of the Explorers Club in New York City. Brainard was eventually promoted to general. Every June, on the anniversary of their rescue, he and Greely would together eat one of the meals they had planned in the Arctic.

21

Andrée didn't ride in a balloon until he was thirty-eight, in 1892. He went up with Captain Francesco Cetti, a Norwegian. In addition to being a balloon pilot specializing in demonstrations, Cetti was a mind reader and a starvation artist. In 1885 he had performed for the Swedish royal family a display of "mind-reading and thought transmission." Two years later, at the Aquarium Theatre in London, he conducted a starvation performance that lasted thirty days, during which he was allowed only water, but as much as he wanted. He ate his last meal, some raw meat with champagne, in front of a thousand people. He began flying balloons in 1890.

Cetti described Andrée aloft as "disagreeably calm." Andrée wrote in his journal, "I observed myself as closely as possible in order to learn whether I was afraid or not. I discovered that I was not conscious of any feeling of fear, but that I probably was influenced by it unconsciously. However I could not note any other signs of it than that I surprised myself holding fast to the stay ropes, although these were the part of the entire outfit in which from the beginning I felt the least confidence. Later I remembered that I had thought them weak and then caught hold of something else. It took a few seconds before this reasoning seeped through. As I let go of the ropes I thought: 'I must have been afraid.' But I felt no sense of dizziness, not even when I leaned over the railing at the highest point of our flight and looked right down into the deep."

After two flights with Cetti, Andrée decided that he needed his own balloon. With money from a fund created to further science and the public welfare, he bought one he called *Svea,* after the thistle that is the Swedish national emblem. He made nine flights in *Svea,* all of them alone, sometimes carrying a mirror in order to see whether his face turned different colors at different altitudes.

On his first flight, on July 15, 1893, the balloon rose quickly, then fell and hit the ground, then rose again. The flight lasted about two and a half hours and covered twenty-six miles. At 13,500 feet he could hear dogs barking. Descending, he noticed that as gas escaped, the bottom of the balloon flattened and became like a parachute. After landing he wrote that three seemed the ideal number of people to take part in a balloon trip devoted to science—one person to manage the balloon, one to observe, and one to record the observations.

Andrée's second flight, in August, lasted seven hours and covered sixty miles, during which he rose as high as 11,800 feet. He recorded the temperature and took photographs that were used to correct a map. He also noticed that the balloon fell faster when under the shadow of a cloud.

Andrée's third trip, in October, was the first on which he used guide ropes over water, and it also made him famous in Stockholm. He left early in the morning, with the wind blowing faintly toward the east. By the time he had finished making notes on the weather and the things that he saw, he was over the Baltic Sea, with Sweden receding. He tried to slow the balloon by lowering its anchor. Then he emptied some ballast sacks, tied them to the end of his landing line, and let them drift in the water like a sea anchor. A steamer appeared in his path, and Andrée hoped that he could get the steamer to catch the landing line. From the way the captain of the steamer maneuvered his ship, however, he appeared to believe that he could place himself in Andrée's way and catch the balloon in his rigging. Not only would this be dangerous for Andrée, but if the balloon came too close to the steamship's funnel it would explode and catch fire. Andrée rose clear of the ship, intending to reach Finland.

To make the balloon go faster Andrée tried to haul up the landing line, but couldn't and had to cut it instead. He couldn't lift the anchor either, but let it drag in the water rather than lose it. He headed toward Finland at about eighteen miles an hour. The ships he passed he merely waved to, and they waved back. Around three in the afternoon, realizing he would have to go faster to make Finland by nightfall, he cut the anchor loose. Shedding gas, the balloon rose and fell like a kite in a varying wind. The evening arrived while he was still aloft, and then it grew dark. Above a small island that was hardly more than a rock, Andrée stood on the basket rail, preparing to jump, when the wind shifted suddenly, turning the basket over and throwing him to the ground at 7:18, which he was able to note because the impact smashed his watch. It also dislocated one of his shoulders and broke one of his arms. The balloon sailed away; it was found on an island fifty miles distant. Andrée swam to a larger island where he spent "an extremely unpleasant night." What food he had begun with—three sandwiches, two bottles of beer, two bottles of Vichy water, and some brandy—he had consumed on the trip. Rain fell. At 11:00 the following morning, a fisherman arrived in a rowboat. Andrée asked why he hadn't come sooner, and the man said that when his wife had seen the balloon she had concluded that the Day of Judgment had arrived, and she wouldn't let him leave the house until daylight. Andrée had to pay him to row him to shore. He wrote a telegram to friends to say that he was all right, but the messenger didn't send it until that evening, so it arrived in the middle of the night, and because of the suspense over his disappearance, and the time that had passed, it was printed in a special edition of the papers. The steamer that carried him back to Stockholm was met by three thousand people. He had traveled 170 miles, over ten hours, and used the guide ropes for 120 of them.

22

Leaving the ground on its fourth flight, in February of 1894, the *Svea* was struck by a gust of wind that took it toward an enormous woodpile. Andrée had to throw out so much ballast to avoid the pile that the balloon ascended quickly to a little above a mile before he collected himself and began making notes on the temperature. He eventually rose above two miles, and when he landed he got stuck in a tree. Running back to some of the buildings he had passed over, he met a woman and a boy who had locked themselves in their house and would not come out until he had persuaded them that he was not an apparition or an evil spirit.

On his fifth flight Andrée ascended to fourteen thousand feet, higher than on any of his other flights. Approaching thirteen thousand feet, "the beating of the pulse produced a faint singing noise on the left side of my skull," he wrote. It also gave him a headache. On his sixth, in July of 1894, he used guide ropes and a sail and found that he could steer the balloon at a deviation of nearly 30 percent to the wind. This result, along with his experience over the Baltic, convinced him that a balloon could travel long distances and that it could be made to go where it was wanted to. On this trip Andrée also threw cards out of the balloon asking anyone who found them to send them back to him so that he could tell exactly where he had been. The seventh trip was mostly devoted to notations about the wind and the clouds and the temperature. The eighth lasted three and three-quarter hours and covered 240 miles. For the first time he landed using the rip valve, which let out nearly all the gas in fewer than two minutes. The valve allowed him to stop the landed balloon, instead of having it be dragged by the wind. Sometimes aeronauts landed safely but were injured or killed when their balloon was dragged, and they either fell out of the basket or struck something hard. Andrée made his last ascent in the *Svea* on March 17, 1895. In all he had spent about forty hours aloft and had traveled more than nine hundred miles. In June he sold the *Svea* to an outdoor museum in Stockholm.

23

After giving his speech in Stockholm, Andrée went back to work in the patent office. Money for the voyage arrived slowly. On the tenth of May, Alfred Nobel called on Andrée at work. Eight years earlier Nobel had come to Andrée's office on a matter concerning a patent, and for three hours they had carried on a discussion about "everything between heaven and earth," Andrée wrote, during which they had shared not a single opinion. When Nobel appeared the second time, he asked Andrée if he recognized him, and Andrée said that he remembered their exchange and was prepared to continue it. Instead Nobel said that if the subscription for the balloon trip wasn't closed, he wanted to make a contribution. A week later, hearing from Andrée that money hadn't been coming in quickly, Nobel offered half the amount Andrée needed, so long as the rest could be raised in two months. Andrée took Nobel's offer to the king, who felt that by virtue of their

propinquity the Swedes deserved the honor of discovering the pole and gave him eight thousand dollars. In nineteen days Andrée had all that was necessary.

Andrée's balloon was built in Paris from layers of varnished silk. The upper portion had three layers of silk and the lower, two, which happened to be the formula that John Wise had proposed for his transatlantic balloon. It was ninety-seven feet tall and sixty-seven and a half feet around, and it weighed a ton and a half.

On the top was a coverlet to keep snow from settling, and to inhibit the sun from heating the gas. A net made of hundreds of ropes enclosed the balloon. From their ends hung the bearing ring, which was made from American elm, and from the ring hung the basket, a rectangular box made from willow and Spanish cane on a frame of chestnut, because iron or steel would have affected the magnetic instruments they carried for science. Where metal was necessary, Andrée used, if possible, bronze, copper, or aluminum, which are not magnetic. The basket frame was wrapped in sailcloth covered with tar. Customarily the bottoms of baskets were rounded and given to tipping over when they were dragged, but Andrée made the bottom of his basket flat, with one edge rounded and the opposite one straight. Food and anything else vital was typically carried in the basket, but Andrée had everything essential stowed in pockets strung between the bearing ropes (because of the instruments, the food was stored in copper tins). Knowledgeable people said that if the basket struck the ground and turned over, the aeronauts would fall out and the balloon would sail away with their food and tools. Andrée was more concerned about coming down in the water and drowning. By placing his provisions in the ropes, he and the others could climb into the bearing ring if the basket landed in the water, then cut the basket loose and ride off. If they hit the water and were flooded but able to rise without having to shed the basket, they could open two valves in the floor to drain it.

Above the basket was a platform where two men could work and keep watch, while one slept in the basket on a horsehair mattress encased in reindeer hide. Hydrogen is explosive. To heat water and cook, Andrée had a stove, invented by a friend, that could be lowered from the basket until it hung about twenty-five feet beneath it. It was lit from the basket through a tube. A mirror placed by the stove allowed someone in the basket to see if the flame had lit. Blowing down a second tube put it out.

From the bearing ring, eleven ropes hung, like tails on a kite. Eight of these, called ballast ropes, were stationary. Each was seventy-seven yards long and weighed 110 pounds. If the balloon sank low enough, the ropes would touch the ground, thereby losing some of their weight and helping to prevent the balloon from sinking farther. If the balloon rose, more rope rose with it, slowing the ascent.

The other three ropes, called the guide ropes, were meant to drag on the ground. Each had an upper section of hemp and a lower one of coconut fiber, which were joined by metal ends that threaded together. Fifty-five yards from the end, each also had a weak point, so that one that caught fast would snap. If a rope that had snapped snagged a second time, its parts could be unscrewed by a mechanism in the gondola. If both methods failed, Andrée, in 1897, had a device made of brass that slid down the rope and stopped where he wanted. Inside were two knives that cut the rope when a gunpowder charge was set off.

To prevent the guide ropes from tangling, each was a different length—one was 1,205 feet, one was 1,042, and one was 1,017. Altogether they weighed sixteen hundred pounds. The first of the guide ropes' two functions was to help control the balloon's elevation. In clouds or fog the hydrogen would contract, and the balloon would sink. Sunshine caused the hydrogen to expand and the balloon to rise. Andrée planned to travel above the fog and below the clouds, which would preserve the hydrogen. As with the ballast ropes, the more of the guide ropes that touched the ground, the less they weighed on the balloon.

The guide ropes' second purpose was to help steer the balloon. A balloon traveled where the wind blew. The only means of controlling its course was to throw out an anchor and wait until the wind shifted, or to climb and hope to find a wind going the way the pilot wanted to go. Since a balloon couldn't go faster than the wind, and therefore against it, the only way to steer was for the balloon to travel slower than the wind and to use a sail. Andrée's plan, tested on the *Svea,* was to slow the balloon with the guide ropes. A sail could then propel the balloon aslant to the wind, "just as it does with a sailing boat," Andrée wrote. A course deviating as much as twenty-seven degrees from the wind was possible—he said that he once got forty degrees in the *Svea.* To run before the wind, the sail would face it. To run obliquely, the balloon would be turned by moving the guide ropes with a pulley, which rotated the balloon on its vertical axis. Andrée's balloon had three sails—two small ones on either side of a large one that hung from a bamboo mast just below the balloon, between the net and the bearing ring. In all the sails covered about eight hundred square feet, a quarter of the circle of the balloon. The sails on the *Svea* had been roughly one-eighth the size.

Whether Andrée made it or not depended largely on the ropes' working well, so they were tested thoroughly at two factories in Stockholm, one that made fuses and one that made horseshoes. They were dragged over the ground and over ice, and mounted on a flywheel and turned by a steam engine for twenty-six hours, at the end of which no signs of friction were found. To waterproof them they were pulled through barrels of petroleum jelly mixed with animal fat, palm oil, wax, and paraffin. Andrée decided the best mixture was three-quarters petroleum jelly and one-quarter fat.

To send messages Andrée planned to take carrier pigeons, given to him by the Swedish newspaper *Aftonbladet.* Fastened to the pigeon's middle tail feathers were parchment cylinders into which *Aftonbladet* meant Andrée to insert dispatches. Aboard the balloon was room for thirty-six birds in small baskets.

Andrée estimated that the balloon included seventy innovations, thirty of which he thought of himself. His three sledges, made of ash, had a second pair of runners on the top of the sledge, so that if a runner broke, the sledge could be turned over. "I get as good as two sledges out of one," he said. In addition, he had a tent made from balloon silk. The floor was three layers thick, and the cover was a single layer varnished with the mixture that was used on the balloon's envelope. The last large piece of equipment was a boat that was assembled from a wood frame covered with layers of silk. To test it Andrée went out on Lake Mälaren with nine people aboard. Finally, although neither Andrée or his crew was much of a skier, he brought skis, in case they made pulling the sledges easier.

According to the head of the company that supplied their

food, they were to bring "every kind of steaks, sausages, hams, fish, chickens, game, vegetables and fruit." It was the first polar expedition to bring lozenges of concentrated lemon juice to prevent scurvy. In addition they had about fifty-five pounds of "thin chocolate cakes, mixed with pulverized pemmican." This was wrapped in parchment and packed inside airtight boxes. Should they have to land and travel over the ice, they had food for two years, assuming that they would also kill bears. Every piece of equipment was marked "Andrée's Polar Expedition 1896." On wood it was printed, on metal it was engraved, and on the balloon, the tarpaulin covering the basket, and the ballast bags it was painted. Where there wasn't room it was abbreviated. In addition the underside of one wing of each pigeon was stamped "Andrée."

The balloon was made by Henri Lachambre in May of 1896. It was inflated and displayed for a week in a gallery at the Palais du Champ de Mars. Beside it was a balloon sufficient to carry two people, which according to one observer resembled "a small piece of sugar by the side of an egg." Thirty thousand people came to see it, among them the president of France, who later sent "to the three courageous men of this daring enterprise the warmest wishes for a successful outcome, which will be followed with the greatest and most intense attention in France as well as everywhere else in the civilized world."

24

The notion that natives of the Arctic had a hundred words for snow is apocryphal. Mariners, however, had many names for types of ice. Greely's book had a glossary of terms, and Sir Clements Markham, the English explorer who had risen from the audience to admonish Andrée, also defined terms in a lexicon called "Ice Nomenclature," which appears in "The Antarctic Manual for the Use of the Expedition of 1901."

New ice was called young ice. Old ice was from at least the previous year. Paleocrystic ice took years to form, which was apparent from its greater thickness. Bay ice, or harbor ice, formed each fall. Pieces of it were drift ice. A small collection of drift ice was a patch, and a large one was a pack. A close pack was dense; an open pack had lanes of water running through it. Sailing ice was ice in an open pack that allowed room for a ship to pass. Round pieces of pack ice were pancake ice: collisions had softened their edges.

Long narrow trains of broken ice were streams. Stray bits of ice, usually small and sharp or with other irregular features, "the wreck of other kinds of ice," according to Markham, was brash ice, rubble or mush. Brash ice mixed with saltwater was sludge ice. Pen-knife ice had been covered with water that had left columns, sometimes pointed, six to eighteen inches tall that were painful to cross. Rotten ice was honeycombed from melting unevenly. The water from its surface was ablation.

A floe was a plain of harbor ice. An indentation or a bay in a floe was a bight. Above the floes, like hills, rose hummocks, formed by pressure and also called pressure ice. A hummock might be as much as fifty feet tall, and some were reported as reaching a hundred. The boundaries of a floe could be seen from a crow's nest. A floe that extended beyond the horizon was a field. Field ice, made of paleocrystic ice, could be as thick as twenty feet. A sufficiently agitated sea could make a field appear to undulate, to move in "swell-like ridges, as if our ice was a carpet shaken by Titans," an American explorer named Elisha Kane wrote. For Kane the sight was startling, since for weeks the ice had appeared "as unyielding as the shore." Now it had taken "upon itself the functions of fluidity, another condition of matter."

Ice attached to the shore was land ice, or fast ice. Ice that lay against the shore and didn't move with the tides was an ice foot. The border between an ice foot and the migrant ice was a tidal crack. An iceberg forced ashore was a floeberg. Floeberg was also the name for a paleocrystic iceberg in the shape of a cube. A piece of ice that rose abruptly to the surface from beneath a floe was a calf. A tongue was a calf still attached to a floe. In smooth water a tongue could usually be seen to some depth. Chinese walls were the cliffs at the end of a glacier whose foot was in the sea. Island ice covered an island, as in the case of White Island, where Andrée was found.

Field ice was saltwater ice. Ice from fresh water, such as snow that had melted, was sweet-water ice. According to Julius von Payer, sweet-water ice was "hard as iron, and so transparent that it is scarcely to be distinguished from water." By the end of summer, when the air was damp, snow covering the ice became grainy, with the grains sometimes larger than beans, Payer said, and in a wind they made a rustling sound like sand. In winter the snow in some places was hard as rock and elsewhere as fine as dust or sugar. "Where it lies with its massive wreaths frozen in the form of billows, our steps resound, as we walk over them, with the sound as of a drum," Payer wrote. "The ice is so hard it emits a ringing sound." In bitter cold, butter got hard as stone, meat needed to be split like cordwood, and mercury could be fired from a gun. In parts of Siberia milk was sold in pieces. One explorer's account describes Eskimos using the cold for revenge on wolves that had attacked them. Into the ice the Eskimos set several sharp knives with their blades upright; then they covered the blades with blood. The wolves licked the blades and cut their tongues, but felt nothing because of the cold. Their own blood on the blades kept them licking "until their tongues were so scarified that death was inevitable."

A ship attempting to make headway in the ice was said to be boring. If its crew had tied ropes to a stationary object such as an iceberg and were pulling, they were warping. A ship caught in the ice had been nipped and was beset.

Distant light reflected from ice looked different from light reflected from water. A dark storm-colored horizon denoted open water and was a water sky. A yellow brightness over a horizon meant the distance was dominated by ice, and the effect was called an ice blink. A mariner seeing an ice blink knew that there was no point trying to force his way to open water: nothing lay before him but more ice.

One of the reasons that there are so many terms for conditions of ice is that the mariners observing it were often trapped in it, and had nothing to do except look at it. With the close attention of naturalists, they described how it formed. From the edge of old ice "threads like a spider's web" ran toward the middle of young ice, according to J. Y. Buchanan, in the *Antarctic Manual,* causing the young ice to thicken into a substance that was "thin and pasty," and that followed "every surface movement of the water." Even in the worst cold, however, it would not support a man before thirty to thirty-six hours. Then it sank under his weight, without breaking. "It gives the impression that one is walking on well-stretched leather," Buchanan wrote. For as long as two weeks it will bend more than break under pressure. The flexibility is a matter of the salt water, which freezes differently from fresh water. The concentrations of brine never freeze, and give the ice its pasty texture. "On walking over such a surface, so long as no fresh snow has fallen on it, one is astonished to find that every step one takes remains impressed on the white surface."

The ice also made a lot of noise. A crewmember of Nordenskiöld's ship, the *Vega,* wrote, "The song of the sea ice is a very peculiar one, and can scarcely be described so as to convey any clear idea of its nature. It is not loud, yet it can be heard to a great distance. It is neither a surge, nor a swash, but a kind of slow, crashing, groaning, shrieking sound, in which sharp silvery tinkling mingle with the low, thunderous undertone of a rushing tempest. It impresses one with the idea of nearness and distance at the same time and also that of immense forces in conflict. When this confused fantasia is heard from afar through the stillness of an Arctic night the effect is strangely weird and almost solemn, as if it were the distant hum of an active, living world breaking across the boundaries of silence, solitude and death."

25

There is more than one North Pole. Andrée's destination, the geographical North Pole, from which all directions are south, is at ninety degrees N. The north magnetic pole, which wanders, and is the pole toward which the compass needle points, is situated in northern Canada. It was first reached in May of 1831 by an English naval officer named John Ross. The north geomagnetic pole is on the northwest coast of Greenland. The geomagnetic pole marks the intersection between the earth's surface and the axis of a magnet that might be placed in the center of the earth. The pole that represents the longest distance from any land in the Arctic is the pole of relative inaccessibility. Until 1926, when an airship flew over it, it was the pole of inaccessibility. Sometimes also called the pole of ice, it is halfway between Franz Josef Land and Ellesmere Island. The first person to arrive there on foot, an English explorer named Wally Herbert, visited in

1968, on his way to the geographical pole. The north pole of cold, where temperatures sometimes fall near ninety below Fahrenheit, is along the Indigirka River, in Siberia, between the villages of Tomtor and Oymyakon, which are the coldest inhabited places on earth.

When Greely, in his speech before Andrée's in London, spoke of the Arctic's "startling by astounding phenomena that appeal noiselessly to the eye," he was describing capacities of the Arctic air, which because it contains so much moisture and there are so many ice crystals floating in it, and because it is often so still, produces many arresting effects. One of these is parhelia, the appearance of additional suns, sometimes in the shape of a cross. The apparitions are also called sun dogs. Payer reported seeing eight of them once, in April 1872, from the deck of his ship, the *Tegetthoff.* He wrote that they came before episodes of driving snow and were so frequent that they no longer amused him.

Another peculiar condition of Arctic light is the Novaya Zemlya effect, in which the sun appears on the horizon as a rectangle and sometimes in the shape of several hourglasses stacked on top of one another. The actual sun is below the horizon, but its image is projected through layers of thermoclines—zones of differing temperatures, that is.

Perhaps the most eccentric quality of the air is its capacity to produce refractions—changes in the appearance and proportions and placement of objects. Sometimes a refraction duplicates an object, like a reflection in water, and sometimes it bizarrely obscures the object's identity. Elisha Kane wrote one evening in 1854 on his ship: "Refraction again! There is a black globe floating in the air about 3 degrees north of the sun. What it is you can not tell. Is it a bird or a balloon? Presently comes a sort of shimmering about its circumference, and on a sudden it changes shape. Now you see plainly what it is. It is a grand piano, and nothing else. Too quick this time! You had hardly named it, before it was an anvil—an anvil large enough for Mulciber and his Cyclops to beat out the loadstone of the poles. You have not got it quite adjusted to your satisfaction, before your anvil itself is changing; it contracts itself centerwise, and rounds itself end-wise and, *presto,* it has made itself duplicate—a pair of colossal dumb-bells. A moment! And it is the black globe again.

"About an hour after this necromantic juggle, the whole horizon became distorted: great bergs lifted themselves above it, and a pearly sky and pearly water blended with each other in such a way, that you could not determine where the one began or the other ended. Your ship was in the concave of a vast sphere; ice shapes of indescribable variety around you, floating, like yourself on nothingness; the flight of a bird is as apparent in the deeps of the sea as in the continuous element above. Nothing could be more curiously beautiful than our consort the Rescue, as she lay in mid-space, duplicated by her secondary image."

To mariners the icebergs were immense and ghostly forms, both substantial and ethereal. "There was something about them so slumberous and so pure," Kane wrote, "so massive yet so eva-nescent, so majestic in their cheerless beauty, without, after all, any of the salient points which give character to description, that they seemed to me the material for a dream, rather than things to be definitely painted in words." Once a boat had entered their region it was surrounded. In 1818, the explorer Sir William Edward Parry, off Greenland, began counting the ones in his vicinity and gave up at a thousand.

Light went through icebergs as if through a prism, turning them different colors according to its angle of entry. "On our road we were favored with a gorgeous spectacle, which hardly any excitement of peril could have made us overlook," Kane wrote. "The midnight sun came out over the northern crest of the great berg, our late 'fast friend,' kindling variously colored fires on every part of its surface, and making the ice around us one great resplendency of gemwork, blazing carbuncles, and rubies and molten gold."

Not only sunlight made the ice seem ghostly. Of a night landscape Kane wrote, "A grander scene than our bay by moonlight can hardly be conceived. It is more dream-like and supernatural than a combination of earthly features.

"The moon is nearly full, and the dawning sunlight, mingling with hers, invests everything with an atmosphere of ashy grey. It clothes the gnarled hills that make the horizon of our bay, shadows out the terraces in dull definition, grows darker and colder as it sinks into the fiords, and broods sad and dreary upon the ridges and measureless plains of ice that make up the rest of our field of view. Rising above all this, and shading down into it in strange combination, is the intense moonlight, glittering on every crag and spire, tracing the outline of the background with contrasted brightness, and printing its fantastic profiles on the snow-field. It is a landscape such as Milton or Dante might imagine—inorganic, desolate, mysterious. I have come down from the deck with the feelings of a man who has looked upon a world unfinished by the hand of its Creator."

The unfinished aspect, the whiteness and immensity of the Arctic, unnerved Herman Melville, who had been among ice as a whaler. *Moby-Dick* has a chapter called "The Whiteness of the Whale," in which Ishmael tries to locate the horror inspired by the whale's abnormal color. Within it, he wrote, "there yet lurks an elusive something in the innermost idea of this hue, which strikes more of panic to the soul than the redness which affrights in blood." Rather than purity or innocence, he sees the cold whiteness of the dead and the color of the shroud they are wrapped in. "Therefore, in his other moods, symbolize whatever grand or gracious things he will by whiteness, no man can deny that in its profoundest idealized significance it calls up a peculiar apparition to the soul."

26

Andrée was to be accompanied to the pole by Nils Eckholm, the meteorologist who had led the Swedish delegation to Spitsbergen in 1882, and Nils Strindberg, a physics professor. Eckholm was forty-eight and had been born in the central Swedish region of Kopparberg, to a father who like Andrée's was a pharmacist. He had been a physicist before he got interested in meteorology, and he was regarded as an authority on Arctic weather. He and Andrée had not gotten along especially well in Spitsbergen, but he wrote that "bonds of friendship were formed that did not break." Whether they had kept in touch afterward is no longer known, but in 1893 Andrée had written to Eckholm about balloon flights and asked for advice about meteorology. He signed on in 1895. He was tall, with a high forehead; deep-set, owlish eyes; and he wore wire-rimmed glasses. The lower half of his face was obscured by a beard and mustache so thick that they looked like a mask.

Nils Strindberg was born in Stockholm and was twenty-four. His father, Oscar, was a wholesaler who published verse under the pseudonym Occa. Oscar's cousin, and Nils's godfather, was the writer August Strindberg. Strindberg's mother, whose name was Rosalie, was also from a venerable Stockholm family. She and Oscar had three other sons, Tore, who became a sculptor; Sven, an art dealer; and Erik, an architect, who later lived in America. Nils was the second child, and his father's favorite.

Strindberg had, according to a report from the period, "a fine open countenance" and "the frank ingenuous manners of a boy." The writer went on to describe him as taking "immense delight in the prospect of the voyage to the Pole." When he was asked how he and the others would know that they had arrived at the pole, he said, "The instant the south wind becomes a north wind." He went to an elite boys' grade school in Stockholm that was also attended by members of the royal family. As an adolescent he learned to take photographs and to play the violin. His favorite opera, which he saw with his parents when he was twenty, was Léo Delibes' *Lakmé*, a melodrama set in India during the mid to late nineteenth century. It is the period of British rule, and they have forbidden Hindus to practice their religion. A British soldier falls in love with Lakmé, the daughter of a Hindu priest who regards the courtship as an affront. The priest stabs the soldier, whom Lakmé takes to the forest and nurses to recovery. She is off getting holy water to sanctify their relationship when a British soldier arrives and persuades his friend that his duty to his regiment is greater than his obligation to Lakmé. The love affair is over, and Lakmé takes poison rather than live under the shadow of scandal. Strindberg learned pieces from it on the violin.

He went to high school at Stockholm College, where his best subjects were physics and chemistry. At home in his room, he had a laboratory where he carried out experiments. He became close to a professor named Svante Arrhenius, who was later on the committee that helped establish the Nobel Prizes and then won the Nobel Prize in Chemistry in 1903. Arrhenius was the first scientist to suggest that changes in the amount of carbon dioxide in the atmosphere would alter the earth's temperature: the greenhouse effect.

In 1893 Strindberg received a degree from Uppsala University, and over the next two years he published papers about electricity and electrical circuits. In 1895 he got a position as an amanuensis, an assistant, in physics at Stockholm University, and in the fall he joined Andrée's expedition.

How he did isn't entirely clear. He may have won a competition. It is also possible that he heard Andrée deliver a talk about his plan and spoke to him about it, or that Arrhenius knew Andrée and introduced them. Strindberg was interested in flying machines and had written a paper about Samuel Pierpont Langley, a rival of the Wright brothers. Langley had launched two aircraft from a catapult in the Potomac River in the weeks before the Wright brothers' flight, and both had crashed. Strindberg's paper went unpublished.

Strindberg's mother had recently died, apparently of stomach cancer, and his father was not convinced that his son should join Andrée. He wasn't opposed so much as skeptical and needed more than once to be assured that Andrée's plan was practical. His first impression of Andrée, he wrote, was of a man with a mustache, a bent nose, a handsome mouth, and large slender white hands. His dress was proper and his bearing strong, and he seemed happy and to joke a lot. He was the sort of person one could listen to for hours, Oscar thought. He noticed that all the women in his family were immediately sympathetic to Andrée, even the ones who weren't usually well disposed toward others, and he felt sure that his wife would have liked him. "And after talking to him," Oscar wrote, "would have felt considerably less fear than she would otherwise have for this venture."

Andrée arranged for Strindberg to travel to Paris to learn to fly a balloon, and he went in March of 1896. He was befriended by famous aeronauts who took him to cafés, and by a rich industrialist who had him to his estate, where they hunted rabbits (the party shot sixty, six of which were Strindberg's). For breakfast he served Strindberg wild boar tails, which were roasted, and which Strindberg enjoyed but thought tasted strange. In the evenings he liked to walk on the boulevard St.-Germain and say *Bonsoir* to the people he passed. He visited the Eiffel Tower and wrote home that he was more disconcerted by being high up in the tower than when aloft at the same height in a balloon. He went to the opera to see *Faust* and was impressed, but thought that Stockholm had at least as good an opera company. He saw the Lumières' famous moving image of the train arriving at La Ciotat. He stayed at a pension where one of the other guests was a young American woman making a tour of Europe with a chaperone. Her name was Jones. She had long blond hair piled high on her head like Marie Antoinette, beautiful hands, and slightly round cheeks. You start an interesting conversation with her and immediately fall deeply into it, he wrote to one of his brothers. After what he called the polar trip, he thought he might visit her, or that she might come to Sweden with her chaperone. On the last evening before she left, he took a photograph of her and sent it to his brother. Before his second ascent, as he was preparing to launch, she handed him an album and asked him to write verses in it when the balloon had reached its maximum altitude, which disconcerted him, but he did it. "What does this mean in America?" he asked his brother. "Does it mean anything at all?"

He went to tea at the studio of a woman sculptor named Matton, who had a friend named Miss Rudbeck, who was a physical therapist. The three of them then went to the Grand Café, where someone mentioned a club, Café de la Mort, which had an atmosphere like a spookhouse. They went looking for it and found it in a basement on the boulevard de Clichy, with a green electric light at the entrance. The room they walked into was lit by a chandelier of candles that Strindberg sketched in a letter to his brother. The chandelier consisted of human skulls arranged in a ring and attached to a spine that connected to the ceiling. The tables were coffins, and the waiters were dressed as hearse drivers and monks. The drinks were served in glasses that had *Bacilles* written on them—bacilli being a genus of bacteria—and were called drinks of death.

On the walls were portraits that changed abruptly, so that the figures became skeletons, and everyone was given a candle and led into a vaulted cellar room, where a skeleton occupied a niche, as in a catacomb. In front of the skeleton was the image of a saint. Everyone placed his candle next to the saint, then took a seat on a bench. In another niche was an empty coffin. A young man, likely a plant, volunteered to be wrapped in a shroud and placed in the coffin. In his place a skeleton suddenly appeared and the coffin withdrew into the wall while organ music played. Strindberg wrote that a magic lantern—a projector, that is—had been used to accomplish the trick.

From the cellar everyone went to a room that was decorated with symbols of death and another skull-and-spine chandelier. The room had a small stage. A young woman volunteered to sit on a chair, and a ghost walked toward her and kissed her, an effect that Strindberg thought had been produced with a mirror. Finally a young woman began a striptease. As she lifted her chemise, the lights went out. The women thought it was a little vulgar, Strindberg wrote, but they couldn't help laughing.

One evening Nils also met his godfather, who was living in Paris while one of his plays was being produced. August's family later developed the impression that he, and not Nils, was the aeronaut. This had partly to do with Oscar's having sent his son Sven, in Helsinki, a telegram asking him to come home to a party for Nils, who was leaving for the pole. The telegram was delivered instead to one of August's sons. In *The Inferno,* a kind of diary, August wrote, "May 13th.—A letter from my wife. She has learned from the papers that a Mr. S. is about to journey to the North Pole in an air-balloon. She feels in despair about it, confesses to me her unalterable love, and adjures me to give up this idea, which is tantamount to suicide. I enlighten her regarding her mistake. It is a cousin of mine who is risking his life in order to make a great scientific discovery."

After the balloon departed, the painter Paul Gauguin wrote to a friend that "by some circumstance, because I don't read the newspapers, I found out that Strindberg had set off for the North Pole in a balloon, but since then no one had heard anything. But I do hope that he comes back without delay and without having broken his arms and legs."

27

The *Jeannette,* the ship that Greely had been supposed to search for traces of while at Fort Conger, had belonged to James Gordon Bennett, Jr., the New York newspaper publisher who in 1871 had sent Henry Morton Stanley into Africa to find David Livingstone. In 1879 Bennett had sent George de Long in the *Jeannette* to find the pole. The *Jeannette* became stuck in the ice, drifted for nearly two years, was eventually crushed in a hurricane off the Siberian islands, and abandoned while it slowly sank. Twenty of its crew of thirty-three, including de Long, died in the retreat. Some of them drowned when their lifeboat capsized, and the others starved or froze trying to reach native towns in Siberia. In 1884 relics from the *Jeannette* washed up on the southwest coast of Greenland—on the other side of the world, that is. The *Danish Geographical Journal* published a partial inventory:

1. A list of provisions, signed by De Long, the commander of the Jeannette.
2. A MS. list of the Jeannette's boats.
3. A pair of oilskin breeches marked "Louis Noros," the name of one of the Jeannette's crew, who was saved.
4. The peak of a cap on which, according to Lytzen's statement, was written *F. C. Lindemann* [a misprint, since the crewman, who was saved, was F. C. Nindemann].

In 1884 a professor named Henrik Mohn gave a talk at the Scientific Society of Christiania, in Norway, in which he said that he believed that the relics had drifted on a current that crossed the pole. From Mohn's observations the Norwegian explorer Fridtjof Nansen, who had been the first to cross Greenland, conceived the idea that he could strand in the ice a specially made ship—one that would be "small and strong as possible—just big enough to contain supplies of coals and provision for twelve men for five years," he wrote—and be carried in it to the pole.

The ships that had gone to the Arctic had all been conventional ones. They had been reinforced with timbers and iron, but many were still crushed once the ice pinched them. They were too long and narrow, and their sides were too steep for the assault. Nansen's ship would have smooth, gently sloping sides, so that when gripped, the ice could not take hold; instead of being crushed the ship would rise. "The whole craft should be able to slip like an eel out of the embraces of the ice," Nansen wrote.

August or early September would be the time to sail as far as one could into the pack by the New Siberian Islands and moor between floes. The ship would be a sort of floating boarding-house, a barracks, from which the crew could go out on the ice to make scientific studies and notes. If the ice did manage to damage the ship fatally, its demise would happen slowly, leaving time to move all its supplies onto a floe he would have chosen earlier. Those people who thought Nansen's plan had a flaw tended to think that there were islands around the pole that had bays into which his boat would drift and never get out. Nansen believed that the pole was surrounded by water.

Nansen called his ship the *Fram,* which translates as forward. It looked like a bathtub toy—Nansen said it resembled half a coconut. It was 138 feet long and 36 feet wide, with three masts, the tallest of which was a little more than 100 feet. The hold was so intricately reinforced that it looked "like a cobweb of balks, stanchions, and braces." To keep the ship from heeling too much, the bottom was flat. Nansen knew the *Fram* was too wide to sail well—and it didn't. The first heavy sea poured over the decks while the *Fram* rolled on its beam and all the cargo on the deck washed around, and some of it went overboard.

One of Nansen's emphatic critics was Adolphus Greely, whom Nansen referred to as "the leader of the ill-fated expedition generally known by his name." In a piece in *The Forum* magazine, Greely wrote that it struck him as "almost incredible" that Nansen's plan "should receive encouragement or support. It seems to me to be based on fallacious ideas as to physical conditions within the polar regions, and to foreshadow, if attempted, barren results, apart from the suffering and death among its members." Nansen, he went on, "has had no Arctic service; his crossing of Greenland, however difficult, is no more polar work than the scaling of Mt. St. Elias"—a mountain on a boundary between Canada and the United States. Greely doubted that any hydrographer would take seriously Nansen's theory of the polar currents, or any Arctic specialist endorse his plan. He said that Nansen would not be able to build a ship that could sustain the pressure of the ice, mocking him—as he mocked Andrée—by saying essentially that sharp minds had spent a great deal of money trying and would have succeeded if the task were possible. Arctic exploration was "sufficiently credited with rashness and danger in its legitimate and sanctioned methods, without bearing the burden of Dr. Nansen's illogical scheme of self-destruction," Greely wrote.

28

The *Fram* left Norway with thirteen men in June of 1893. Wherever it stopped, people stared at it and then at the crew. In *Farthest North,* Nansen's account of the trip, he wrote: "We were looked on somewhat as wild animals in a menagerie. For they peeped unceremoniously at us in our berths as if we had been bears and lions in a den, and we could hear them loudly disputing among themselves as to who was who, and whether those nearest and dearest to us whose portraits hung on the walls could be called pretty or not." As Norway fell behind, the last figure Nansen saw was a man fishing in the light of the early morning, an image he regarded as emblematic.

The *Fram* entered the ice at the end of September and was not always carried north. Sometimes it went south and even east, the way it had come. At one point Nansen calculated that the pace it was traveling would have them home in eight years. Sometimes the grinding and shifting of the ice was so loud that they had to shout to be heard above it.

In case they had to abandon the ship and make their way home on the ice, they brought sled dogs, which were nearly wild and killed one another if not watched. " 'Job' is dead, torn in pieces by the other dogs," Nansen wrote in October. "He was found a good way from the ship, 'Old Suggen' lying watching the corpse, so that no other dog could get to it. They are wretches, these dogs; no day passes without a fight. In the day-time one of us is generally at hand to stop it, but at night they seldom fail to tear and bite one of their comrades. Poor 'Barabbas' is almost frightened out of his wits. He stays on board now, and dares not venture on the ice, because he knows the other monsters would set on him.

There is not a trace of chivalry about these curs. When there is a fight, the whole pack rush like wild beasts on the loser."

After the sun disappeared for the winter—"a flattened body with a dull red glow, but no heat"—they had the company of the moon, "which goes round the sky night and day." Every now and then the ice parted briefly, and they floated in open water. They lowered pails to the bottom and pulled up mud and emptied out the creatures it held, "chiefly starfish, waving starfish, medusæ (*Astrophyton*), sea-slugs, coral insects (*Alcyonaria*), worms, sponges, shell-fish, and crustaceans," which they preserved in spirits.

Ships in the Arctic became a species of dungeon once the winter arrived. Having been built for waters where the climate was moderate, they weren't well insulated. Vapors from cooking and the men's breathing turned to ice on the walls once the warmth from the cooking had dissipated. When the interior warmed again, the ice melted. Water seaped into the crews' beds and their clothes, then froze once it got cold again. Since the ships had no portholes and a candle might start a fire, the crews lived mostly in darkness. The cold caused them to withdraw into the holds and their beds for weeks, which made everything worse.

Nansen planned for all these circumstances. Heavily insulated, the *Fram* was always warm, and well lit. More than a typical Arctic ship it was a men's club. No one had ever sailed to the Arctic in comfort before.

29

Nansen and Andrée were inspired by visionary theories they were willing to risk their lives to test. Nansen's method involved refining hundreds of years of efforts by thousands of men. He had read all his predecessors' accounts and from everyone's failures he had culled the flaws and corrected them. Nothing could happen to his ship that he wasn't prepared for. He had practically engineered the risk out of his voyage. Furthermore, having crossed Greenland, he knew how to live outdoors in the Arctic, and not simply in a house with other researchers and plenty of fuel and food.

Different from Nansen, Andrée was a pioneer, a futurist. Men had not been sailing balloons to the Arctic for centuries. Almost nothing of what others had accomplished was helpful to him, unless he came down on the ice. Both men desired acclaim, but the pole figured differently to each of them. Nansen hoped to own a contemporary feat, the discovery of the pole, the permanent farthest north. His attempt had a backward-looking cast, a retinue, a history, annals, and an archive. By better preparation and a brilliant intuition, he hoped to surpass the caravans of sledges and fleets of ships that had tried the same thing he was trying. If the others had only known what I know, he might have thought. Years had to pass before other aviators could look back at Andrée's attempt and say, If only he had known. Andrée was the first to try a novel task. For Nansen the pole was primary, and for Andrée too, but he also wanted to prove that men could travel long distances in the air. Andrée never wrote down what had moved him so profoundly to hazard his life. His manner was terse and reserved—"He was a typical Swede," is a remark one often hears about him—and he was not given to confession. He seemed to feel that he had no need to explain himself, or perhaps that confession was undignified. However, Nansen, who had a touch of the extrovert, the buttonholer, and was a natural-born, if slightly fancy, writer, unburdened himself while unsettled one night by the *Fram*'s capricious progress.

"Here I sit in the still winter night on the drifting ice-floe, and see only stars above me," he wrote. "Far off I see the threads of life twisting themselves into the intricate web which stretches unbroken from life's sweet morning dawn to the eternal death-stillness of the ice. Thought follows thought—you pick the whole to pieces, and it seems so small—but high  above all towers one form. . . . *Why did you take this voyage?* . . . Could I do otherwise? Can the river arrest its course and run up hill? My plan has come to nothing. That palace of theory which I reared, in pride and self-confidence, high above all silly objections has fallen like a house of cards at the first breath of wind. Build up the most ingenious theories and you may be sure of one thing—that fact will defy them all. Was I so very sure? Yes, at times; but that was self-deception, intoxication. A secret doubt lurked behind all the reasoning. It seemed as though the longer I defended my theory, the nearer I came to doubting it. But *no*, there is no getting over the evidence of that Siberian drift-wood."

30

The days passed half-idly with tasks and diversions. One night a member of the crew came down to report a more than usually glorious appearance of the aurora borealis, and the rest of them went up to observe it. "No words can depict the glory that met our eyes," Nansen wrote. "The glowing fire-masses had divided into glistening, many-colored bands, which were writhing and twisting across the sky both in the south and north. The rays sparkled with the purest, most crystalline rainbow colors, chiefly violet-red or carmine and the clearest green."

On the Christmas of 1893, Nansen thought of the families who would be worrying over his and the crew's well-being. "I am afraid their compassion would cool if they could look in upon us, hear the merriment that goes on, and see all our comforts and good cheer," he wrote, and then he reported the day's menu:

1. Ox-tail soup;
2. Fish-pudding, with potatoes and melted butter;
3. Roast of reindeer, with peas, French beans, potatoes, and cranberry jam;
4. Cloudberries with cream;
5. Cake and marchpane (a welcome present from the baker to the expedition; we blessed that man).

In January he wrote of a plan that he had brooded on for some time and that was now beginning to possess him: to depart from the ship with a companion and on sledges try to reach the pole. "It might almost be called an easy expedition for two men," he wrote. The plan kept him awake, so that a day later he wrote, "Perhaps my brain is over-tired; day and night my thoughts have turned on the one point, the possibility of reaching the Pole and getting home. Perhaps it is rest I need—to sleep, sleep! Am I afraid of venturing my life? No, it cannot be that. But what else, then, can be keeping me back? Perhaps a secret doubt of the practicability of the plan. My mind is confused; the whole thing has got into a tangle; I am a riddle to myself. I am worn out, and yet I do not feel any special tiredness. Is it perhaps because I sat up reading last night? Everything around is emptiness, and my brain is a blank. I look at the home pictures and am moved by them in a curious, dull way; I look into the future, and feel as if it does not much matter to me whether I get home in the autumn of this year or next. So long as I get home in the end, a year or two seem almost nothing. I have never thought this before."

Two days later he dreamed that he had reached the pole but had seen only ice, and when people asked what it was like, "I had no answer to give," he wrote. "I had forgotten to take accurate observations."

As the new year bore on, he found his thoughts interrupted by images of home. Sometimes when he was absorbed in work, he would hear the dogs bark, then think, Who is coming? before he remembered where he was, "drifting out in the middle of the frozen Polar Sea, at the commencement of the second long Arctic night."

The sybaritic life of the crew led Nansen to wonder what would happen if they actually had to retreat. He began having every man snowshoe for two hours, then one day they tried hauling a sledge weighing 250 pounds. When one of the men pulled it, "he thought it was nothing at all; but when he had gone on for a time he fell into a fit of deep and evidently sad thought, and went silently home. When he got on board he confided to the others that if a man had to draw a load like that he might just as well lie down at once—it would come to the same thing in the end."

31

In November of 1894, on a walk in the evening on snowshoes with Otto Sverdrup, the second in command, Nansen confided his desire to leave the ship for the pole, or as close as he might come to it. Sverdrup, he wrote, "entirely coincided." Nansen and a companion would leave with twenty-eight dogs and a ton of provisions and equipment. The pole was 483 miles away. Without knowing exactly how the dogs would do, Nansen hoped he could reach it in fifty days. For years he had studied other expeditions and felt "enabled to face any vicissitude of fate."

Not long after talking with Sverdrup, though, Nansen read again an account of a sledge journey by Payer and felt sobered. "The very land he describes as the realm of Death, where he thinks he and his companions would inevitably have perished had they not recovered the vessel, is the place to which we look for salvation."

Three tries were necessary for Nansen and Hjalmer Johansen to get away from the *Fram*. The first time the bracing broke on the sledges. The second time Nansen decided that the loads were too heavy. To the degree that the loads included food, they would diminish, but they might also wear the dogs out first. Nansen brought sufficient food for the dogs to last thirty days. After that he planned to feed the dogs on each other, which he calculated

would allow fifty more days of travel, "and in that time it seems to me we should have arrived somewhere."

The false starts allowed them to refine their wardrobe. They began in wolfskin, but it made them sweat, which made the clothes heavier. When they took them off, the garments froze and were difficult to get back on. They decided to wear layers of wool, through which their sweat could evaporate. To protect themselves from wind and "fine-driven snow, which, being of the nature of dust, forces itself into every pore of a woolen fabric," they wore canvas overalls and a canvas pullover with a hood, "Eskimo fashion." Their boots they stuffed with sennegrass, which absorbs moisture. At night the sennegrass had to be pulled apart and dried against their bodies. Underneath wolfskin mittens they wore wool ones, which also had to be dried against the skin, and felt hats under hoods. They slept in a double sleeping bag, which was lighter than two single ones and let their bodies share their heat.

"Something which, in my opinion, ought not to be omitted from a sledge journey is a *tent*," Nansen wrote. His were made from silk and had canvas floors, and he banked them with snow against the wind. In a medicine kit he carried chloroform for an amputation; and cocaine for snowblindness. He also had drops for toothache; needles and silk for stitching cuts; a scalpel; splints and plaster-of-Paris bandages for a broken bone; and "laudanum for derangements of the stomach."

With three sledges and twenty-eight dogs, he and Johansen got away for good on March 14, 1895, when it was forty-five below zero. For more than a week they made about fourteen miles a day; on their best day they did twenty-one. It never got much warmer. They killed their first dog on March 24. Skinning him was difficult. When the parts were given to the other dogs, many of them refused to eat, but they got over it. "They learned to appreciate dog's flesh, and later we were not even so considerate as to skin the butchered animal, but served it hair and all," Nansen wrote.

Even with dogs, sledging was so hard that sometimes they fell asleep as they traveled. They woke when they fell over. Their coats when they sweated froze hard, so that wearing them became like wearing armor, and the coats made a cracking sound when they moved. An arm of Nansen's coat chafed one of his wrists nearly to the bone. Someone under grave stress often has dreams that continue the text of the day. Nansen would sometimes be awakened by Johansen calling in his sleep to the dogs, "Get on, you devil, you! Go on, you brutes!"

The dogs were used cruelly. "It makes me shudder even now when I think of how we beat them mercilessly with thick ash sticks when, hardly able to move, they stopped from sheer exhaustion," Nansen wrote. "It made one's heart bleed to see them, but we turned our eyes away and hardened ourselves."

By the first week of April, Nansen realized that the ice was too rugged and rough to cross, and that the pole was unreachable. They turned back on April 9. They had been killing the dogs with knives, which was disagreeable; now they tried strangling them. They would walk a dog behind a hummock and use a rope, which took so long that they had to resort to the knife anyway. The ammunition they might have used they had to conserve. Each dog subtracted made hauling the sledges harder.

Two months passed and they were still on the ice. Desperately hungry, Nansen wondered if they should eat the dogs that were left and haul the sledges themselves. The dogs were so exhausted that they sometimes fell down and were dragged in their traces. From the blood of one they made a porridge.

Toward the end of June, they had begun to travel through leads in the kayaks they had brought, with the dogs aboard. A seal rose close to them, and they managed to kill it, which gave them food for a month, raising their spirits. "Here I lie dreaming dreams of brightness," Nansen wrote.

32

On July 24, for the first time in two years, they saw something other than "that never-ending white line of the horizon"—land. "We had almost given up our belief in it!" Nansen wrote. They had seen it earlier on several occasions, slightly darker than the ice and rising above it, but had concluded that it was a cloud. It seemed close enough that they thought they might reach it that afternoon. Instead it took thirteen days.

On August 3, a Saturday, Nansen wrote, "Inconceivable toil. We never could go on with it were it not for the fact that we *must.*" Two days later Johansen was picking up a rope by his kayak when he saw something crouched by one end of the boat and thought it was a dog. Instantly "he received a cuff on the ear which made him see fireworks." It was a bear, and the blow knocked him on his back. Johansen grabbed the bear by the throat. Meanwhile, Nansen, who had his back to them and hadn't seen the attack, was trying to pull his sledge and kayak out of the water. Johansen called out, "Take the gun," which was in the kayak. Nansen turned and saw Johansen on the ground, and lost his grip on his kayak, which slipped into the water. He was struggling to recover it, when he heard Johansen say quietly, "You must look sharp if you want to be in time." The dogs distracted the bear briefly, and Nansen's shot hit it behind one ear. From its tracks they could see how it had stalked them.

On August 7 they finally stood at the edge of the ice. "The large head of a seal came up, and then disappeared silently; but soon more appeared. It is very reassuring to know that we can procure food at any minute we liked." Two dogs were left, one on each sledge, but there was no room to carry them on the kayaks—beforehand they had traveled through leads, but now they would be crossing open water. "We were sorry to part with them; we had become very fond of these two survivors. Faithful and enduring, they had followed us the whole journey through; and, now that better times had come, they must say farewell to life. Destroy them in the same way as the others, we could not we sacrificed a cartridge on each of them. I shot Johansen's, and he shot mine."

That evening, having reached the island, Nansen wrote, "The delight of the feeling of being able to jump from block to block of granite is indescribable."

In the following days they shot several walruses, which were disgusting to dress. As the dead animals floated in the shallow channels, Nansen and Johansen had to lie on them and reach with their knives as far as they could beneath the water. Getting wet and cold was disagreeable, but the worse part was being soaked by the blubber and the blood while wearing clothes that they would have to wear all winter.

In September they collected stones for a hut. With a spade they constructed from a walrus shoulder blade tied to a broken snowshoe shaft, and a mattock made from a walrus tusk fastened to a sledge crosstree, they dug a foundation three feet deep. The gaps between stones they stuffed with moss and dirt. Across the roof they stretched walrus skins, which were frozen; one of the skins had to be thawed in water before it could be bent. From the ends of the skins they hung stones to stretch them. Now and then they were interrupted by a bear's appearing or some walruses to shoot. The finished hut was ten feet long and six feet wide and just barely tall enough for them to stand. For months they hardly left it.

On Christmas Day the weather was so fine, with nearly no wind, that Nansen described it as provoking a feeling like "the peace of a thousand years." The northern lights that evening were "a bright, pale-yellow bow." They "smouldered for some time, and then all at once light darted out westward along the bow; streamers shot up all along it towards the zenith, and in an instant the whole of the southern sky from the arc to the zenith was aflame."

For diversion they thought about food or taking a bath. "When we wanted to enjoy a really delightful hour," Nansen wrote, "we would set to work imagining a great, bright, clean shop, where the walls were hung with nothing but new, clean, soft woolen clothes, from which we could pick out everything we wanted. Only to think of shirts, vests, drawers, soft and warm woolen trousers, deliciously comfortable jerseys, and then clean woolen stockings and warm felt slippers. We would sit up side by side in our sleeping bag for hours at a time, and talk of these things."

On New Year's Day of 1896, it was forty-one degrees below zero, and Nansen's fingers got frostbite. He and Johansen spent the winter making new clothes, including socks from polar bear skins, and a new sleeping bag, also from bearskin, since parts of their new clothes had come from the old bag's blankets. "There was not much variety in our life," Nansen wrote. They tried to clean themselves with warm water, using moss as an abrasive. When that didn't work they tried scraping the dirt from their skin with a knife.

In May they emerged and took photographs of their hut and wrote an account of their voyage thus far:

Tuesday, May 19, 1896. We were frozen in north of Kotelnoi at about 78 degrees 43' north latitude, September 22, 1893. Drifted northwestward during the following year, as we had expected to do. Johannessen and I left the *Fram,* March 14, 1895, at about 84 degrees 4' north latitude and 103 degrees east longitude, to push on northward. The command of the remainder of the expedition was transferred to Sverdrup. Found no land northward. On April 6, 1895, we had to turn back at 86 degrees 14' latitude and about 95 degrees east longitude, the ice having become impassable. Shaped our course for Cape Fligely; but our watches having stopped, we did not know our longitude with certainty, and arrived on August 6, 1895, at four glacier-covered islands to the north of this line of islands, at about 81 degrees 30' north latitude, and about 7 degrees E. of this place. Reached this place August 26, 1895, and thought it safest to winter here. Lived on bear's flesh. Are starting to-day southwestward along the land, intending to cross over to Spitzbergen at the nearest point. We conjecture that we are on Gillies Land [another name for White Island].

Nansen signed the note and put it in a brass tube that had been part of their stove, shut up the tube with a wood plug, and hung it by a wire from the rooftree. Then they started walking. Having had so little exercise over the winter, they found the sledges heavy. Aboard their kayaks one day they pulled up to a floe to rest and got out, and when they weren't looking the wind took the kayaks, which were lashed together. Nansen swam after them. The closer he got to them, the stiffer with cold he became. When he was finally able to grab hold of them, he had hardly the strength to pull himself aboard. To paddle back to the floe he had to make two strokes off the side of one kayak, then step across to the other kayak and make two strokes there, while the wind went through his clothes. Two auks landed on the bow, and wanting them for a meal, he shot them both with one bullet. On the shore Johansen, hearing the gunshot and seeing Nansen paddle toward the birds, thought that Nansen had gone insane. When Nansen made it back to the floe, he put on dry clothes, and they spread the sleeping bag on the ice and Johansen covered him with the sail and whatever else could be found. He fell asleep while Johansen prepared the auks, and when he woke he was warmer, and they ate the birds and some soup.

Often their kayaks were followed by walruses. One rose up beside Nansen and struck the boat with its tusks. Nansen hit it in the head as hard as he could with his paddle, but before he could reach his gun, the walrus submerged. Nansen heard water coming into the kayak and managed to get to a floe, where the kayak started to sink. He and Johansen got it out of the water and saw a six-inch tear. Nansen felt sure that the animal had meant to harm him.

On the seventeenth of June, camped on land, Nansen rose to make breakfast. He walked to the edge of the ice for some fresh salt water, and while watching birds, heard what he thought was a dog barking. He decided it had been the birds. "Then the barking came again, first single barks, then full cry." Johansen also thought it was birds. After breakfast Nansen found tracks that might have belonged to a fox. It didn't seem possible that a dog could have been so close to them in the night and made no noise. He heard the dog again, then saw fox tracks among the other tracks, and noted how small the fox prints were beside them. Then there was a long period when he heard only birds. This was broken by a shout. Nansen ran to the top of a hummock and yelled, but moving among the ridges and icebergs, he saw only white until he made out a dark form: the dog—and, in a moment, behind it, a man. Nansen waved his hat, and the man waved back. Shortly he could hear him speaking to the dog in English. As they drew toward each other, "I thought I recognized Mr. Jackson, whom I remembered once to have seen—" Frederick Jackson, who was exploring Franz Josef Land.

Jackson was wearing a wool check suit and high rubber boots. His face was clean and shaved. Nansen hadn't bathed in a year. His skin in places was black from smoke and soot and seal fat. His hair hadn't been cut, or his beard either. Jackson took him for a walrus hunter who had come to some misfortune.

Nansen raised his hat. They shook hands and engaged in a dialogue by Beckett. "How do you do?" each asked the other.

Jackson said, "I'm glad to see you."

"Thank you, I also."

"Have you a ship here?"

"No, my ship is not here."

"How many are there of you?"

"I have one companion at the ice edge."

They walked a little, inland. Jackson stopped and looked him in the face and said, "Aren't you Nansen?"

"Yes, I am."

"By Jove," Jackson said, "I am glad to see you."

33

Nansen asked how things were at home, and Jackson said that Nansen's wife and child had been fine when he had last seen them two years earlier. Then each of them fired two shots as a signal to Johansen to join them.

Jackson's camp was nearby at Cape Flora. He had gone out on the ice because after he and his companions had finished dinner—their schedule was apparently different from Nansen's—they were sitting in their headquarters, smoking pipes, when the company astronomer put his head in the door and said, "How many of you are here? I see a man on the ice floe." Counting, they realized everyone was present; then Jackson said, "Whoever it is, I am off," and he ran out. One of the company, standing on a hill watching two specks through binoculars, said that the stranger approaching was "jumping about from one ice hummock to another in a marvelous manner." Nansen's nearest relative would not have recognized him, the witness said. "His light hair and mustaches were jet black." He went on to say, "His clothes—the one suit he had worn for fifteen months—were stiff with blood and oil with which his face and hands were also covered."

Jackson's party made them dinner—roast loon, green peas, jam tart, cheese, and preserved fruits, served with port, sherry, and whiskey—and Nansen felt the cares of the past three years fall away from him. He was handed a soldered tin box that held letters from Norway, which he opened, he wrote, "with a trembling hand and a beating heart." After reading the letters, "a delightful feeling of peace settled upon the soul." Having spent three weeks trying to reach the pole, it had taken him fourteen months to return.

Within a week, while still at Cape Flora, he heard that Andrée was nearby, on Dane's Island, "waiting for wind to go to the Pole in a balloon," he wrote. "If we had pursued our course to Spitzbergen, we should thus have dropped into the very middle of all this."

34

When Andrée, Strindberg, and Eckholm left Göteborg for Dane's Island aboard the *Virgo* in June of 1896, forty thousand people saw them off. Of those who had helped him, Andrée said that if he died in the attempt, "the last thought that at least I will have is what a pity I was not able to thank them." Before going aboard he wrote to his mother. "Don't be uneasy, dear, your heart is close beside me," and on the *Virgo* he read her last letter. She always worried that something would happen to him, but he had assured her that he was safe in the air. "I am so dissatisfied with myself for having been such a poor, weak creature on that diffi-cult day of leave-taking," she wrote. "But there is *one* thing I wish you to bear in mind, and that is this: if when you return I am no longer here, you must not be depressed by thinking that your grand enterprise has had the *least* influence on my having gone the way of all flesh. . . . And now, my thanks for all you have been to me!"

Andrée reached Spitsbergen on June 21 with fifty-one people, including scientists and carpenters. The following day he spent looking for somewhere to build the balloon house. He chose a place close to the shore where the ground had no ice, and there were mountains on three sides—the balloon would depart to the north over the water. Nearby was a small house built in 1888 by an Englishman named Arnold Pike, who had sailed among the islands and had given Andrée permission to use the house.

The *Virgo* anchored about 150 yards offshore, at the edge of the ice; then, using pine from northern Norway, the crew built a railway to connect to the land. The first items to be unloaded were the equipment and ingredients for the hydrogen. Some of it was hauled over the railway using tackles and pulleys, and some came ashore on rowboats and a small steamer finding its way through leads in the ice, a few of which had been opened with dynamite. Next came the parts of the balloon house. There was rain on Midsummer Eve, the solstice, which is a traditional Swedish holiday, but they celebrated with a party where speeches were delivered, Strindberg played the violin, and a dog did tricks.

Carpenters raised the balloon house, while others among the crew placed the guide ropes in asphalt tubs filled with petroleum jelly and tallow and let them soak for fifteen hours. They ran the ropes through their hands to strip off the excess coating; mostly this was done by Strindberg and Eckholm. Then they attached the ropes and the drag lines to the stern of the steam launch and pulled them through the harbor to determine the effect of their weight. They also filled a small balloon made from goldbeater's skin—the outer membrane of a calf's intestine, which is used in making gold leaf—and let it go, but it rose straight above them, into the clouds, so that they couldn't tell how it had behaved or even what direction it had taken. One evening Andrée and the others practiced splicing lines and tying knots "so we won't be too clumsy in such things." To a friend he wrote, "No problems are weighing on our minds." All that remained was to "travel to the Pole. Nobody on board appears to have got the idea that this will meet with any difficulties." Andrée was pleased at superintending all the work. "It is great to hypnotize on a large scale," he wrote.

On July 11, after Andrée completed his watch aboard the *Virgo* at two in the morning, he went ashore and climbed into the basket, which had been hung so that it could sway in the wind. He had brought with him a copy of Nordenskiöld's book, *Journey of the Vega*, which he read a few pages of and then placed "on the book-shelf which had newly been set up. In this way I consecrated, as well as I could, the new vessel."

By the third week of July the balloon house was finished. Heavy felt covered the floor and the walls; the roof was made from cloth, and the windows from gelatin. The balloon was unpacked and examined for tears, and then it was laid out. The following day it snowed, and the day after that the balloon was inflated. All of Europe and much of America were following Andrée's mission, and steamers and schooners carrying reporters and tourists began arriving. Almost daily, for two hours in the morning and two in the afternoon, Andrée gave lectures for them, which he enjoyed. Dispatches were sent to the wider world. A paper in Philadelphia wrote that "the daring of the aeronauts and the extremely novel enterprise in which they risk their lives give to Andrée's departure something of the interest

which attended the sailing of Columbus's ships upon their immortal voyage. It is impossible, however, to suggest historical parallels to his curious journey."

The balloon had been filled for three days, when Eckholm said there was a strong odor of hydrogen in the house, and that gas had caused the balloon's cover to rise and flutter in the wind. Beneath the cover they found leaks they varnished. Andrée wrote a friend that as soon as the cover was restored, it would be time to leave. "After that, I and others must accept what the forces of nature choose to do. We shall, of course, use all our strength to the end, but this, despite all is only a drop in the ocean, once the balloon has been released."

They needed a southerly wind, but the wind blew mainly from the north or northwest, mostly weakly, and sometimes hardly at all. The *Virgo* was insured until August 20. To reach Sweden by then, it would have to be loaded by the fourteenth.

That morning a ship with three masts anchored about a mile offshore. As it swung on its line Strindberg wrote, "it showed itself in clear profile." He and Andrée and Eckholm were taken toward it in a launch. "We used the binoculars until our eyes began to hurt," Strindberg went on. They thought they knew who it was, "But we did not yet dare to believe it," he wrote. "As we came to 500 meter's distance the name began to appear and I was the first to confirm that it was Fram! It was like a dream. What a strange coincidence, what a peculiar twist of fate!"

They waved their hats and gave four cheers. Andrée made no note of the occasion, but it is not unreasonable to assume that as he approached the ship he was uneasy. If it turned out that the *Fram* had reached the pole, his own voyage would be superfluous. On the other hand, if the *Fram* hadn't made it, he might prove that three years of effort could be bettered in a week. At the gangway ladder, according to Strindberg, Lieutenant Hansen told them something that Andrée couldn't have foreseen—"the

sorrowful news regarding the fate of Nansen and Johansen"—
that they had left the ship for the pole and not been heard from.
("Yet hope still remains," Strindberg wrote.) From Captain Sverdrup, Andrée heard that the *Fram* had not traveled the course it
had hoped to; it had zigged and zagged with the pack, heading
mainly west, and never very far north, and been released above
Spitsbergen. Nevertheless, Nansen might still return having
reached the pole.

The *Fram* left the following day, and a few days later, in
Tromsø, met up with Nansen and Johansen, who had been traveling on Jackson's boat. Meanwhile, Andrée wrote, "Today we
sharpened the scissors, with which the balloon will be cut apart."

35

On August 16, Andrée sent a telegram announcing that the expedition was returning, having not gotten a favorable wind. The
next day at ten in the morning the balloon valves were opened,
and by five it had been deflated. "Like a rag the proud airship
sank to the floor," Andrée wrote. The correspondent for *Aftonbladet* described the mood on the island as "quite depressed."
The hydrogen plant was dismantled, and its parts were stored by
Pike's cottage, and the walls of the balloon house were taken
down and stored on the beach. Andrée thought that forty people
could put the house back up in three or four days, compared
with the thirty-five days it had taken to build it. More days could
then be devoted to waiting for the wind.

Nowhere does Andrée write that he was affected by Nansen's
return, but his feelings toward him were apparent when he con-

cluded his speech in London in 1895 by saying, "Is it not more probable that the north pole will be reached by balloon than by sledges drawn by dogs, or by a vessel that travels like a boulder frozen into the ice?" The sentiment, however—provoked by nationalism—that Nansen had won by traveling farther north than anyone else, and Andrée been defeated, was circulating. The Norwegian novelist Alexander Kielland wrote that Nansen's return "was a blessing for the entire country," Sweden's rival. "Even the Swedes had to contribute to the splendor with their 3 wind bags who returned home with the balloon between their legs."

Andrée's plan had relied on ships and sledges having failed, but Nansen had shown that each could at least still come close. What was needed, some said, was not a balloon but an icebreaker. In addition Nansen's intrepidness cast a shadow of hesitancy, even cowardice, over Andrée's return. Furthermore, some people asked what Andrée, in a sprint, might learn that Nansen on a long tour hadn't. One observer wrote of Andrée's changed circumstances, "Instead of the original jubilant expectations, he is now surrounded by mistrust and indifference on many sides."

By the end of August, Andrée was back in the patent office. While the world had Nansen lead parades and gave him honors, Andrée sat at his desk. A reporter walking down the street in Stockholm with him in September was surprised at how few people noticed him. "It is strange to see how little known this man was amongst his own townspeople, there was not a hat that was lifted for his sake, nobody who passed turned around and whispered, 'This was Andrée who walked here.' "

36

Over the winter Nansen and Andrée exchanged letters. Nansen felt that Andrée's voyage was dangerous, and he hoped, perhaps from self-interest, that he wouldn't try again. "I believe Macbeth's golden words could be placed on your banner," Nansen wrote. " 'I dare to do all that may become a man; Who dares do more is none.' It is in drawing this boundary that true spiritual strength reveals itself." Andrée wrote back, "Since I have proven that I am capable of returning, I am greatly tempted to do just the opposite."

Andrée's backers were still eager to help him. Baron Oscar Dickson who had also supported Nordenskjöld wrote, "Please bear in mind that those of us who have contributed to the expenses for this year, have a preferred right to subscribe to the next try." Alfred Nobel offered to pay for another balloon, but Andrée said that he didn't think that a better balloon could be designed or built. "The balloon is, with regard to its construction and fabrication, as far as I understand, as good as it could be made," he wrote Nobel. To another friend he wrote that all care had been taken to prepare the balloon. "All that is humanly possible has been done when it comes to sealing," he wrote, "the best-known method for the seams has been used, and the most renowned manufacturer employed, what is left?" Because the balloon had been heavier than he had expected, though, he had a band three feet tall added to its equator so that afterward the balloon was a hundred feet tall and sixty-seven and a half feet across at its widest point. The first version had been spherical, and the new one was slightly elliptical.

Andrée had been home from Dane's Island only a little longer than a month when his difficulties deepened. In a speech to the Society of Physics, Eckholm revised several of his predictions about the balloon and the trip. Friction from the drag ropes would cause the balloon to travel half as fast as Andrée had forecast, Eckholm said, meaning the trip would take twice as long. Andrée had allowed a margin of safety that was five times greater than the time he thought necessary—that is, for the six-day trip that he had assumed, he had designed a balloon that he believed could stay in the air for thirty days. Now that the trip, according to Eckholm, would take twelve days, the balloon had to remain aloft for sixty days, which almost everyone doubted it could. On Spitsbergen, according to measurements Eckholm had made, it lost gas at a rate that suggested seventeen days was more reasonable. Eckholm's measurements had been difficult to interpret, however. The balloon seemed to lose gas erratically, which didn't seem probable. Not until he was back in Sweden did he learn that Andrée had been having the balloon refilled.

Eckholm also told his audience that his calculations had predicted a straight path for the balloon, but now he thought that it would travel "in many crooks," which would double and perhaps triple the miles needed to reach land on the far side of the pole. Furthermore clouds would force the balloon to travel close to the ground and slowly, and sometimes even to stand still.

Andrée had been content to arrive at the pole in the air and return over the ice if he had to, but Eckholm felt that such a trip was beyond even Nansen's capabilities, and probably out of the reach of an engineer, a meteorologist, and a physicist who had no experience of traveling in the Arctic and hadn't trained for it, either. He wanted the balloon somehow made able to travel faster or the envelope made less permeable, which was not simple, considering that in applying nine miles of thread, needles had passed through its surface something like eight million times.

Andrée defended himself by saying that he thought that the balloon would not lose gas as quickly as Eckholm predicted, and that as time passed it would lose less. Moreover, once enough gas had been lost, one of the guide ropes could be discarded, with the result that the balloon would be lighter and go faster. Furthermore, even seventeen days was more than sufficient for their purposes. Strindberg added that the polar ice would cause less resistance to the ropes than snow, and that if a strong wind blew at the start they would cover more ground than forecast and so spend less time in the air.

Eckholm didn't merely give a speech, he also went to the Stockholm train station to meet the king's train and tried to persuade him to withdraw his support. When the king, surprised to see him, asked where Andrée was, Eckholm disingenuously said that he had expected him to be present, and that he must have been delayed, meaning to imply that he was acting with Andrée's approval. Eckholm also wrote to some of Andrée's backers, hoping to convince them that Andrée's flight was impossible.

On September 19, Strindberg wrote his brother Sven, "Next year's expedition is likely to involve a great change. Eckholm is probably not coming along! This is still being kept secret. This is the situation. Eckholm, upon return, has blamed Andrée for failing to keep his promises regarding the balloon's permeability and poses preconditions for his participation, by which Andrée neither can nor wishes to abide as they show a mistrust of Andrée's integrity. Moreover, he has behaved in a tactless manner in several ways, partly by waiting alone with tail wagging to receive the king as he returned from Norway, partly by secretly going against agreement and writing to the expedition's patrons in an attempt to depict it as dangerous. Judging by appearances it seems as though he is suffering from pressures from his wife's side and now wants to emerge from the situation with dignity intact. All of this is between us!"

Scholars have speculated that Eckholm was trying to preserve his reputation. If Andrée discovered the pole without him, Eckholm would look like a turncoat and a coward. If the trip were abandoned for practical and technical reasons, though, he might appear to be a rational man of science who had the courage to put the well-being of others above his own ambitions and whose caution had saved lives.

A few weeks later Andrée wrote Eckholm, "While it should be unnecessary to put forward a question that had already been asked and answered in the affirmative, I feel forced, due to circumstances that you know, to once again ask for your kind and definitive answer to my question, if you are willing to accompany next year's balloon expedition." Eckholm wasn't. Andrée also suspected that Eckholm's wife had influenced him. In 1895 Eckholm had married a woman named Agnes Boden, who was thirty years old and taught singing and piano.

To a friend Andrée wrote that he didn't think Eckholm's leaving would matter. "I don't think that this needs to give any reason for anxiety regarding the expedition, at least I do not have this feeling."

37

At the end of October 1896 Andrée wrote to Alfred Nobel, "I have the sad duty to inform you that Strindberg has rushed ahead and got engaged." He added that he hoped that Strindberg would not "follow Eckholm's example." He felt he could only wait, however, to learn "what face his fiancée, Miss Anna Charlier, will show."

As a teenager, visiting a family in the country, Strindberg had hidden with some friends behind bushes to spy on several girls who were swimming naked in a lake. When the boys jumped out, the girls ran away. One of the girls was Anna Charlier, whose father was the postmaster in a town nearby. Charlier played piano, and during the years afterward she and Strindberg sometimes played duets. In October, having returned from Spitsbergen, Strindberg was visiting friends in Johannesdal, outside Stockholm. He was staying on an estate belonging to the wife of a rich industrialist who had started a school for disadvantaged children. Charlier was a governess there. Strindberg was having a show of photographs from Spitsbergen. A large group of friends spent the day together then had dinner, and afterward there was music, and they danced. By the time the evening was over, Strindberg saw Charlier differently from the way he had before.

Sixteen days later she was a guest at a dinner at his family's house. Strindberg had decided that he would ask her to marry him, but being one of the hosts, he was so busy that he didn't have the chance. She left behind a pair of galoshes, and the next morning, rather than have a servant return them, Strindberg took them to her. She wasn't up, and he had to wait. They went to a café where they were constantly interrupted by people they knew. Charlier was returning that afternoon to Johannesdal on a boat. On the way to the harbor Strindberg was finally able to ask her.

In the weeks after, Strindberg agonized over how far it was proper to let matters proceed. On one occasion she sat on his lap and her keys fell to the floor, and in reaching for them he was able to touch her leg. "We long for consummation," he wrote, "and every time we meet it becomes more affectionate. What is the right thing to do? Hold back or give in? I must restrain myself. That is unconditionally the right thing to do."

Meanwhile, from one of the hundreds of young men who

applied to replace Eckholm, Andrée received a letter, "I herewith apply for the position vacated by Dr. Eckholm as the third man on the polar expedition proposed by the Chief Engineer for the next year. I am 26 and a half years of age and have a healthy and strong physique. I have passed my matriculation and graduated from the Royal Technical High School's Department of Highways and Hydro-engineering. Your obedient servant, Knut Hjalmar Ferdinand Fraenkel, civil engineer."

Fraenkel was tall and strong and loved being outdoors, and Andrée liked his straightforward manner. His father had worked in construction for the state railway, which meant that he was moved to wherever rails were being laid. Since lines were most often built through countryside, Fraenkel grew up playing in the woods and the fields, and, according to the portrait of him that appears in *The Andrée Diaries,* he developed "a physique which became uncommonly strong and hardy." He is sometimes described as the expedition's packhorse. He didn't drink or smoke. "Excessive enjoyment is the death of pleasure," is a remark he was fond of.

In school, the report continues, "Knut Fraenkel was no bookworm." His best subject was gymnastics. When he was a boy an "eye-affliction necessitated his studies being carried on with the greatest caution." His second-favorite subject was history, and he liked reading about kings and royal exploits, especially those of Charles XII, the king of Sweden from 1697 to 1718, who fought a number of wars. When a friend came to visit Fraenkel in Stockholm and asked to see the town, Fraenkel took him to a park where there was a statue of Charles and had his friend take off his hat before it. Fraenkel had hoped to become an officer, but "an operation for a nervous complaint which he was obliged to undergo had compelled him to change his plans, and to enter the Royal Institute at Stockholm in order to study for his father's profession." He had gotten in the second time he applied. When he joined Andrée's expedition he was hoping to find a place among the engineering corps of the "Road and Water Construction" department.

Fraenkel had never been to the Arctic, and he hadn't flown in a balloon, either. In April and May of 1897, he went to Paris as Strindberg had and made ten flights, meaning that altogether, by the time the expedition left, its three members had made twenty-seven flights. On one of Fraenkel's flights the balloon fell so fast that when he and the others threw out sand they were using as ballast it hit them in the face. Fraenkel regarded the experience as fine sport.

Either from genuine fondness or because Andrée felt a persistent obligation to put Strindberg's family at ease, he spent a lot of time with them during the winter, which annoyed Gurli Linder, who felt overlooked. In a memoir she published in 1935, she addressed him directly, "That winter the Strindberg family had claimed even more of your presence than before. You did not have as much to do for the expedition at the time. You certainly noticed that it was a completely different circle than that to which you previously belonged. We spoke about this a few times the previous winter. 'You understand that I must show them kindness for Nils' sake. But they are not at all of the same sort as ours.' The host"—meaning Oscar—"was a typical bourgeois Stockholmer from the trade association circle, jovial, well-meaning, slightly well-known and a poor writer of poetry. However, it was a moment in which you were relatively pleased, where you were the main highlight around which everything revolved, for which you were admired and fawned over. In our circle you were just one among many equals, here you were the only one."

Among the regular company at the Strindbergs' was a singer and actress named Ida Gawell, who performed under the name Delbostintan—she was from Delbos—and Linder felt envious of her. "Happy and witty as she was, it was probably she whose company you enjoyed most," Linder wrote, "and this was gratefully used by the circle to bring you together as a couple."

Even so, before he left, she gave him a gold ring with two garnets and a turquoise stone.

38

Over the winter Alfred Nobel died, unsettling Andrée. Then, shortly before the three explorers left for Spitsbergen again, Strindberg's father held a farewell dinner, which Andrée was unable to attend because his mother had died unexpectedly— "from paralysis of the heart," Strindberg's father wrote, meaning a heart attack—and he was attending her funeral. Strindberg's father saw Andrée a week later, as the three were leaving, and wrote that he "was as calm as the summer sea." Privately, though, Andrée grieved deeply. "Now all my personal interest in the expedition has gone," he wrote. "To be sure, I am still interested in carrying out my idea; I have the same feeling of responsibility for my companions, but of the personal sense of joy there is not a trace. The only thread which bound me to the wish to live is cut off. No doubt all those who start on enterprises like mine, having somewhere a purely individual interest, a feeling of happiness at the thought of some one in whose arms they wish to rest after a completed task, where without reserve they can offer themselves, the essence of their battle, the noblest of their joy. In my case it was only to my mother that this individual interest was attached and you can therefore sense, perhaps, what I have lost."

Baron Dickson died also. To Dickson's widow, Andrée wrote, "This is dreadful. Shall I not get any joy from my work? Or does a heavy fate rest over the whole thing?"

Anna Charlier came to Stockholm to spend the last days with Strindberg and his family. It was perhaps during this time that Strindberg took the photograph of her, reclining, that was found in his pocket on White Island. They saw a production of *Lakmé*. The few hours before he left they spent alone. Strindberg was calm until he left his father's house, "when he burst out weeping for a few moments," his father wrote. "He is indeed a man, for he left the dearest he has on earth"—meaning Charlier—"to carry out a great idea, and therefore I do think we shall see him back again."

Charlier held herself intact until she returned to the Strind-bergs' house from the train station, and then she fell into Sven's arms and wept.

The papers published tributes. One said of Andrée, "Yes, it is you, our hero with the old Viking blood in his veins." The explorers took the night train to Göteborg. On the platform the cheer "Long Live Andrée" was raised and repeated twice. On May 18 they departed Göteborg on the gunboat *Svenskund*. The day they arrived in Spitsbergen, May 30, a Chicago paper ran a piece that began, "Andrée's daring in attempting to reach the pole in a balloon is almost certain to cost him his life." This judgment belonged to a polar expert named Lewis L. Dyche, a professor at Kansas State University.

"His expedition, as an example of daring, has never been equaled," he said; "it is a piece of stupendous courage, but nature in its most terrible aspect is against him."

"The theory that the north pole may be crossed in a balloon is extremely fascinating," Dyche continued, "but the difficulties in the way are almost, if now quite, insurmountable. Nansen's drift in his boat through the polar currents was completely practicable beside it. Ice and land are tangible things to travel over, but who knows of the currents of the air?

"Andrée's expedition is most fascinating in its bare possibilities of success, and eclipses that of Nansen in its reckless daring." Even so, "I am afraid that Andrée's attempt will be disastrous, although I sincerely hope he will get through all right and land in America.

"The fascination for polar exploration is marvelous. It is a challenge that nature throws down to man. 'Win the pole,' she says, 'and great will be your prize.' She has awarded prizes for these attempts and the nearer the explorer reaches the pole the greater the prize. Nansen's prize has been world-wide fame and an ample fortune. Should Andrée succeed in reaching the pole

and returning his name will never die and the world will be at his feet. Many men have considered it a prize well worth the attempt."

The year spent celebrating Nansen had included banquets that Andrée and Strindberg and Fraenkel had attended, and Nansen and Strindberg had spoken often enough to become friendly. To Strindberg, Nansen wrote, "It would be idle, my dear Strindberg, to say that I should not feel a passing pang of jealousy if you should reach the Pole ahead of me. Nevertheless, I wish you success with all my heart. Skoal to the Andrée balloon; and may it solve the great problem in safety."

39

Arriving at Dane's Island in a bay filled with pack ice, Andrée searched the shoreline. "It took longer than I had expected to catch sight of the building," he wrote. "But finally the upper poles were visible above the hillside and then I could see the two top storeys. What a happy sight that was!"

According to Strindberg, "The balloon house stood when we arrived, but was so damaged by the winter storms that it was on the verge of collapsing. But one must remember that it was only calculated to remain for one summer. With the aid of tackle and buttresses it was soon fixed, and June 14 we brought the balloon from the 'Virgo.' "

Andrée had also returned with a Swedish military officer named Gustaf Svedenborg, who was an alternate to Strindberg and Fraenkel. Over the following days, to varnish the seams, they filled the balloon with air from a huge bellows. The interior of

the balloon impressed one man who saw it as being "like the cupola of a mighty church." Supervised in turn by Strindberg, Fraenkel, and Alexis Machuron, the cousin of the builder and his representative, eight men, with varnish pots and brushes, went over every seam in the upper half of the balloon (being lighter than air, gas would not escape through a lower seam). "The varnish makes the air very bad," Strindberg wrote, "and after some time one begins to feel a pain in one's eyes."

In the third week of June, they began filling the balloon with hydrogen. "I sit alone in the balloon house with the somewhat more than half-filled balloon beside me," Strindberg wrote. "Hard winds from the NE whistle through the upper parts of the balloon house and in the mountain above. I hold watch beside the hydrogen apparatus, but now I am free from duties as the filling is going well. It is strange to sit here now, once more this year, and to think that this year I am engaged to the best girl in the world, my sincerely beloved Anna. Yes, I may shed a tear when I think of the happiness that has passed and that may never again be returned to me. But what would this matter to me if I merely knew that *she* would be happy. But I know that she loves me, which makes me proud, and that she would be deeply affected by my departure. Therefore I cannot neglect in my sadness to think of her and the happy times we spent together this winter, and in particular this spring. But allow me to hope. The balloon is now varnished and should be much tighter than last year; we have the summer before us with its favorable winds and sunlight. Why wouldn't our mission succeed. This I fully believe."

One of the balloon engineers invented a method for detecting leaks that involved saturating strips of linen with acetate of lead and laying the strips over the seams. Any hydrogen escaping turned the muslin black. "The smallest leakage can be discovered," Strindberg wrote. To carry out part of the task, they had to walk on the crown of the balloon, which, Strindberg said, "only yields imperceptibly." They were unable to finish, however, because they ran out of varnish. Only half of what they had ordered arrived.

Noting the rate at which gas was lost and its effect on the balloon's carrying capacity, Strindberg estimated that, by throwing out ballast, "We will easily float for more than a month. With a fairly strong wind we will reach the pole, or a point near it, in from thirty to sixty hours. Once having reached the northernmost point, we don't care where the wind carries us. Of course we would rather land in Alaska, near the Mackenzie River, where we would very likely meet American whalers, who are favorably disposed toward the expedition. It would really be a glorious thing to succeed so well. But even if we were obliged to leave the balloon and proceed over the ice, we shouldn't consider ourselves lost. We have sledges and provisions for four months, guns and ammunition; hence are just as well equipped as other expeditions as far as that is concerned. I would not object to such a trip. The worst thing is that folks at home will feel uneasy if we don't appear in the fall, but are obliged to spend the winter in the Arctic regions. My body is now in such good condition, and I have got so accustomed to the Arctic life, that a winter up here don't seem terrible at all. One gets used to everything. But the best thing would be to come home in the fall."

40

On July 6, during a storm, the wind blew heavily from the southwest, and even though held by five tons of ballast, the balloon knocked against the walls of the house. At one point twenty sacks of ballast fell from it, and as it surged upward, Andrée was caught in the net and rose with the balloon until he hung upside down. When the storm was over, hydrogen had to be added. Andrée said also that he had noticed shortcomings that needed attention, although he didn't say what they were. "Had they been allowed to remain until the balloon really was to leave," he wrote, "it could easily have happened that it would have been impossible to save the balloon from a shipwreck in the harbour at departure."

Fraenkel and Strindberg thought that the blustery winds were good for leaving, and they began getting the ropes and the basket ready, but Andrée didn't think the winds were dependable. The next day they blew strongly from the northeast, the wrong direction. A few days later Andrée told a journalist that he would not go back to Sweden without having tried to start. At stake were his honor, and Sweden's, he said. Nothing guaranteed that he would reach the high latitudes—indeed, getting the balloon out of the balloon house at all was dangerous—but at least he would have been the first to try using a balloon. He was not, he said, a dreamer or a fanatic, but someone soberly aware of all the dangers and obstacles.

On the eighth of July, the wind blew from the right quarter but too vigorously—it was nearly a gale—then later in the day it came from too far to the west. "If we don't get a southerly wind before the 15th of July," Andrée wrote, "we intend to try with a southeasterly, to be carried north of Greenland, and there possibly utilize the south winds which, according to Lieutenant Peary, are prevalent during the summer."

Later that day he made his last entry before leaving. "Conditions have undergone a considerable change during the last few days," he wrote. "After a month of dry weather we now have mild showers almost every day. The barometer, which previously was very sluggish, now makes quite violent movements and the wind, which hitherto has hardly blown from any direction south of east-west, now sets in from other directions. In the higher air layers, beginning with the height of the nimbus clouds, there appears to be a considerable movement from a more southerly direction. It is characteristic of these new winds that they are puffy, which doesn't appear to be the case with winds from the north. It is evident, however, that we now have arrived at a period of change and that we can hope to get off.

"I have proposed to my comrades that until the 15th of July we are to place quite high demands on the wind which we choose as our traveling wind. But after that date we are going to be content with less satisfactory currents, if they are only of such a nature that they make possible the start itself. For it seems to me that after so much waiting we are entitled, not to say obliged, to make the start. Without the least difference of opinion all three of my comrades agree with me in this respect and we intend to act."

41

Around three in the morning on July 11, the wind began blowing across the bay. By four it was steady from the southwest, and sometimes squalling. The clouds moved constantly north. Two Norwegian sealers arrived looking for safe harbor from a storm, which they expected to last a few days.

Around eight, having rowed ashore with Strindberg, Fraenkel, Svedenborg, the alternate, and Machuron, Andrée said that he would like to brood for an hour, but that Strindberg and Fraenkel should pack their things and finish their letters. Fraenkel wrote, "Dear Mother, time for only a few lines now as we may cast off today. The wind is not the best in direction or strength, but we have waited so long now that we must take this chance. If you hear no more this year we may be wintering in the Arctic. A winter camp on Franz Joseph Land presents no difficulties. I must finish here!"

The sky in the north grew clear while clouds in the south moved quickly, suggesting that the wind blew even more forcefully aloft. Andrée's concern was that the wind was too squally to be trusted. Also, that it might be blowing too strongly for the balloon to get safely out of its house. Finally he asked, "Shall we try it or not?" Fraenkel was not sure; Strindberg said, "I think we ought to try it." Andrée didn't answer, and they went back to the ship. He preferred to wait until the next day, to see if the winds improved. "If we only could get going," Strindberg wrote his father. "Andrée is too careful. The wind has been excellent since 6 a.m. and we have been up on the balloon house measuring the wind. It was 8 metres per second. Andrée thought this to be a bit too much, and became doubtful. But finally I got him to decide

that if the wind did not increase within the next couple of hours we should leave. The officers on board were furious over this lack of firm resolution." Strindberg went on, "And I agree with them. It is disgusting to see."

As soon as Andrée got aboard, though, he told the captain, "My companions insist on starting, and as I have no absolutely valid reasons against it I shall agree to it, although with some reluctance." Then he asked the captain to send all hands ashore to begin dismantling the balloon house.

Andrée did not write his reservations down, so what they were isn't known. A tone of caution seemed to have entered his thinking, though. Perhaps he had come to feel that he wouldn't make it. Or it might also have had to do with his heart's having gone out of the adventure once his mother had died. Or perhaps he was only being practical and wondering, with lives at stake, whether the winds might be more favorable if he were patient.

Strindberg took photographs of the balloon in its house. Then, leaving Andrée and Fraenkel, he rode back to the *Svenskund* for some things he had forgotten and to check his chronometer. Breakfast was on the table when he arrived, and the captain was opening a bottle of champagne. Andrée and Fraenkel had sandwiches later. Meanwhile, over a megaphone, Andrée gave instructions on how to dismantle the house.

To attach the basket to the bearing ring some ballast was removed from it, which caused the top of the balloon to rise slightly above the house, exposing it to the wind. It swung on its moorings, "at times with great violence," an observer wrote. The guide ropes were laid out in coils on the beach. The pigeons were loaded aboard. The aeronauts dressed in their expedition clothes—Andrée and Strindberg in dark blue and Fraenkel in a gray coat with a wolfskin collar. Andrée wrote a telegram to the king, sending "warmest greetings to the fatherland." Lachambre, the Frenchman who made the balloon, had called it *Pôle-Nord,* but Andrée christened it *Ornen,* which translates as "the eagle." He stepped into the basket first. Strindberg asked Machuron if he would give his love to Anna Charlier. Then he set about assuring himself that the camera was working.

"Suppose you alight on the pack ice, far away in the desolate polar regions; what will you do?" a journalist asked.

"We shall do our best, and work our way back as far as possible," Andrée said. "Having during these last years thought, worked and calculated in preparing for this expedition, we have, so to speak, mentally lived through all possibilities. Now, we only desire to start, and have the thing finished some way or other."

The journalist asked when the world might hope to hear from them.

"At least not before three months; and one year, perhaps two years, may elapse before you hear from us, and you may one day be surprised by news of our arrival somewhere. And if not—if you never hear from us—others will follow in our wake until the unknown regions of the north have been surveyed."

They left at two-thirty in the afternoon. First the hawsers anchoring the balloon were cut, so that only three ropes held it. The balloon rose slightly and rolled on its moorings—Machuron wrote that it seemed almost to come to life. "There is profound silence at this minute," he went on. "We hear only the whistling of the wind through the woodwork of the shed, and the flapping of the canvas." Andrée stood in the basket "calm, cold, impassive. Not a trace of emotion is visible on his countenance; nothing but a firm resolution and indomitable will." Three sailors from the *Svenskund* held knives, and on Andrée's count of three, they cut the ropes. "In one second, the aerial ship, free and unfettered, rises majestically into space," Machuron wrote. Leaving the balloon house, the balloon struck something, and the last thing Andrée was heard to say was "What was that?"

Everyone ran from the shed to follow the balloon. Machuron left "through a secret opening I have made in the woodwork, so as to be able to rush to my photographic apparatus and have time to take a few snapshots of this stupendous moment."

The balloon rose slowly and almost erratically to about three hundred feet. It headed northeast, across the harbor, trailing the ballast ropes, which left a broad turning wake. Then very quickly it descended, and the basket struck the water. Andrée threw out eight bags of sand, about 450 pounds, which he would have preferred to keep. Some of the watchers thought that a gust coming over the mountains had forced the balloon to the water. More likely one of the guide ropes had caught on the shore or become stuck while uncoiling. In any case, by the time the balloon had recovered, they had suffered their first misfortune. The guide ropes twisted in such a way that the lower portion of them unscrewed and remained on the ground. Andrée shouted to the sailors onshore while it was happening, but not in time. Without the ropes, Andrée was sailing a free balloon, not one he might steer. Like all the balloonists before him, he had to go where the wind took him.

Machuron stood on the rocks by the water. "Hats and hand-kerchiefs are waved frantically," he wrote. Andrée and Strindberg and Fraenkel appeared to be arranging the sails on the mast. The balloon was traveling about twenty miles an hour. "If it keeps up this initial speed and same direction, it will reach the Pole in less than two days," Machuron wrote. They watched it grow smaller, until, after about an hour, it went over some hills and appeared to be lost. They stood staring at the horizon, Machuron said, and, "For one moment then, between two hills, we perceive a grey speck over the sea, very, very far away, and then finally it disappears.

"The way to the Pole is clear, no more obstacles to encounter—the sea, the ice-field and the Unknown!"

The watchers drew closer together. "We look at one another for a moment, stupefied." Their three friends were now "shrouded in mystery.

"Farewell, heroic scientists!" he wrote. "Our most fervent prayers go with you. May God help you! Honour and glory to your names!"

43

Andrée had predicted the speed of the Arctic wind from the average of readings made by Greely's party at Fort Conger, by the Americans at the other polar station in Point Barrow, his own readings from Spitsbergen, and ones from the Eiffel Tower.

Eckholm, using what findings he had, along with "known laws of the movements of the atmosphere," thought that conclusions could be drawn about what conditions were likely. He believed that several zones of high pressure encircled the pole, while over the pole itself was a zone of low pressure. Passing storms determined the force and direction of Arctic winds. How they operated could be inferred from areas where similar conditions existed.

Eckholm was regarded as the most knowledgeable person in Sweden about Arctic weather. He had concluded that "wind conditions should be especially favourable for such an expedition." To a friend in 1895 he wrote that, given what he regarded as the consistency of the Arctic weather, Andrée's expedition was "no more dangerous than an ordinary long journey by steamship or railroad in civilized countries," so long as "the participants are self-confident, intelligent and cold-blooded persons, who themselves can ensure that everything is in order." When the rewards are much more substantial than the risks, "a clever person plays, but not otherwise."

When Andrée left, no one knew whether the pole was on land, lay within an open sea, or if there were islands around it, or islands with mountains, all of which would influence the weather and the wind. Andrée thought that if he was drawn close to the pole but not over it, he would try to hover close by and make a second approach. In all he might make several. He might also land the balloon to take scientific samples, he said.

44

A few days after the launch Svedenborg, the alternate, visited Oscar Strindberg and Anna Charlier in Stockholm. He told them that Strindberg's last words had been, "Long live Sweden," and he gave Charlier a sandbag that Strindberg had cut loose so the balloon could leave.

Both Eckholm and Svedenborg said that Andrée had suffi- cient rope to repair the guidelines. If he hadn't been able to fix them, however, he was traveling in a balloon whose altitude he wouldn't have been able easily to control, which meant that he wouldn't have been able to manage so efficiently the amount of hydrogen that was lost. The benefit, though, was that as he rose higher the winds would have blown harder.

Four days after Andrée left, a pigeon landed in the rigging of the sealer *Alkin,* near Spitsbergen, folded its head under its wing, and fell asleep. The captain thought it was a ptarmigan, a bird he could eat, and crept close to it and shot it, but it fell in the water.

A few hours later he met another sealer, whose captain said the bird might be related to the Andrée expedition and that there might be a reward for it. The captain of the *Alken* went back and found it. In a tube attached to one of its tailfeathers was a message, dated July 13, 12:30 p.m.: "Latitude 82°2': longitude 15°5' E. good speed to E., 10° south. All well on board. This is the third pigeon-post. Andrée."

According to the coordinates, Andrée had not yet passed the pole, as Machuron had predicted; he had traveled only 145 miles north and 45 miles east, and was heading east instead of north. The two other birds that Andrée mentioned were never found. In the summer the Arctic is full of falcons.

Trying to account for the route that the balloon had taken, Eckholm said that it had likely ascended into a species of cyclone, that is, a whirling storm whose center would have been calm. Using accounts from sealing captains of the weather around Spitsbergen when Andrée had left, Eckholm had concluded that the center of the storm would have been northwest of the island, meaning that the balloon, having been carried north, then northwest, would have stayed at the center of the storm until it picked up a current heading east. That movement agreed with the one that Andrée had described in his message, and it would explain his remark that the balloon was making "good progress eastward." Cyclones, however, require strong winds to form, and those blowing across Spitsbergen might not have been vigorous enough. Andrée might simply have caught winds blowing north and then east.

Regardless of how the route was plotted, they had covered only 120 miles in two days. To reach Siberia or Alaska at that speed would take thirty-three days. Most likely they had landed. Against that possibility, an illustrated notice had been distributed among the captains of the revenue cutters and whalers visiting ports near where Andrée might descend.

153

In the summer of 1897 a balloon (an object like that shown on the drawing) may be seen floating in the air. This balloon will convey a party of three Swedish scientists, who have been making explorations toward the north pole by these means. The Government of Sweden and Norway has requested that the explorers may receive all possible assistance. Natives should therefore be told that the balloon is not a dangerous thing, but merely a mode of conveyance in the air just as a ship is on the water.

Natives should be told to approach the people on it without fear and to give them all the help in their power.

If the balloon is seen only, the natives should be told to communicate the day and hour, the direction and time it was visible, and the direction of the wind.

If the people arrive, having lost the balloon, the natives to be told to give them all possible assistance.

It is requested that the traveler may be supplied with passport and all the official documents, the names being Solomon August Andrée, aged 43; Nils Strindberg, 45 [a mistake]; Knut Hjalmar Ferdinand Fraenkel, aged 27; or one of those replaced by Wilhelm Emanuel Svedenborg, aged 28.

Fourteen days after the launch, on July 25, the *New York Times* reported that two pigeons with messages had turned up in Norway. One message said, "North Pole passed, fifteenth," and the other said, "North Pole 142 W., 47 minutes, 62 degrees," points suggesting that Andrée had reached Alaska. Eckholm said the birds didn't appear to be Andrée's but the paper wrote that the messages implied that "they are probably safe, and will make their way home by way of the Mackenzie River."

July 25 was Anna Charlier's birthday, which she spent with the Strindbergs. In the morning they sailed to an island in the harbor and picked strawberries and, according to Oscar in a letter, "sat down, dreaming, with thoughts on the Pole." In the afternoon they went to the offices of *Aftonbladet,* where Machuron gave

Charlier photographs of the balloon's leaving. They also talked with reporters who had watched the ascent. "There was not *much* news due to all the newspapers had printed," Oscar wrote. They told him, though, that "the loss of a number of drag cables was generally seen as an advantage as this allowed for a start with speed," he said. Finally the reporters gave Charlier Strindberg's violin, some books, and some of his clothes. "You can imagine the impression it made to see all these things arranged," Oscar wrote.

45

Toward the end of July the *Chicago Chronicle* wrote, "Has Andrée crossed the north pole? Has he discovered an open polar sea? These are the questions that the scientific men in every country are discussing. But, aside from the scientific results, the success of the expedition, the most daring in modern times, is of interest to the world at large."

In September, Baron Nordenskiöld, with whom Andrée had first discussed the trip, told a reporter that he was amused more than saddened by the reports of Andrée's death that had begun to appear. "It is my belief that Andrée is at the present moment upon ice which has hitherto been untrodden by the foot of man," he said, and that he expected Andrée to arrive home in the spring, from Siberia.

For months word of Andrée, pieced together from second-hand reports and conjectures, arrived intermittently. Late in November the captain of the *Fiskeren*, sailing near Spitsbergen, saw something large and reddish brown floating about a mile offshore, which he thought was a capsized boat, then later thought might be Andrée's balloon, but he wasn't able to examine it. A sealing captain named Johan Overli, whose ship was the *Swan,* said his crew heard a scream one night off Dead Man's Island, near Spitsbergen. After a brief interval, they heard three more. Overli said the surf had been running too high for him to stop. The *Swan* retreated to a fjord to sit out a storm and was wrecked, and its crew were saved by the *Maygin,* a Norwegian boat. Passing the island again they heard three more screams, but the captain refused to investigate, saying they were birds. From Philadelphia came a report, first published in the Stockholm papers, "The bark Salmia, loaded with cryolite and on its way from Ivigtut, Greenland, has arrived in Philadelphia and brought the information that the natives of Ivigtut report, as of about three weeks later than Andrée's departure, that they saw a balloon traveling at an elevation of about one thousand feet. They watched it for a while. It disappeared, moving in a northerly direction."

In the fall of 1898 a ship captain reported that he had heard from the natives in Angmagssalik, on Greenland, that in late October or early November of 1897 they heard a gunshot one night from out on the ice. Since everyone in the village was accounted for, and since the shot had been heard by several people in several places, they decided that it must have been from Andrée's party adrift on an ice floe.

The first of Andrée's buoys to be found was found on the north coast of Iceland in May of 1899, nearly two years after Andrée had left. It had been jettisoned by Andrée on July 11 at 10:55 at night, after he had been gone about eight and a half hours. "We are drifting at an elevation of about 600 metres," Andrée had written. "All well." Another buoy was found in August of 1900, 1,142 days after Andrée had dropped it, by a woman collecting driftwood in Norway. She thought that it had come ashore recently. "Our journey has gone well so far," Andrée wrote. "We are drifting at an elevation of about 250 meters, with a course which at first was N 10 E True. Four messenger pigeons were sent out at 5:40 P.M. Greenwich time. They flew westerly. We are now over the ice which is much broken up. The weather is beautiful. We are in the highest spirits."

The polar buoy, the one they intended to drop when they passed over the pole, was found on King Charles Land, an island east of Spitsbergen, in September of 1899, with no message. The absence of a message led many people to presume that Andrée had died. The arguments against this included the possibility that he had dropped the buoy in the excitement of passing over the pole and had meant to drop another after it, with the readings of his position, and the second one had not yet been found. Or, from cold or fatigue, he might not have been thinking clearly. Or, for some reason, he might have had only enough strength to lift the buoy over the side and let go of it.

46

Oscar Strindberg wrote in a letter, "And so one has to go on and hope for a year at least; and even after that don't draw too unfavorable a conclusion, for they may have long distances to walk before they reach inhabited places.

"At present I read Nansen's book with great interest, and in my thoughts I place 'the three' in the same or similar situations. Since they have rifles and sufficient ammunition and the necessaries for a journey over the ice and a stay over the winter, I suppose they can do it, although with difficulties to overcome.

"Andrée and Nils, whom I know best, are such characters that, if possible, they make the impossible possible; and they have surely intelligence enough to figure out the best way of getting out of their emergencies. Andrée's ideas and Nils's Anna are two mighty levers and self-protections, and the love of life will help along too."

47

In 1898 word reached Sweden from Russia that Andrée had landed in Siberia, and a journalist named Jonas Stadling, who had been at the launching, went to see if it was true but didn't learn anything conclusive.

Writing in *McClure's Magazine,* Walter Wellman said that there seemed to him to be three places where Andrée might have landed. Wellman was a newspaperman and explorer who tried in 1906 to fly an airship to the North Pole from the place on Dane's Island where Andrée had left from. The engines of his airship failed, however. He thought Andrée might have traveled about five hundred miles east to Franz Josef Land, which he would have recognized in the white landscape "by the black cliffs at the edges of the fjords." Landing there would have meant that he had given up on winds that would take him farther north. A depot had been left for him in a hut at Cape Flora, on the south-eastern end, by Jackson, the man who had encountered Nansen. It included a rifle and four hundred rounds, twelve cans of tobacco, eight gallons of whiskey, salt, coal dust, cheese (damaged by frost, Jackson noted), cans of beef, cases of "rump-steak, veal, and tripe and onions," chocolate, butter, tea, "four dozen fire-bricks," and lime juice. ("He is on a most risky journey—the most so of any that has ever been attempted," Jackson wrote later. "He exhibits great pluck, and I wish him every success in his brave venture.") If Andrée hadn't been able to reach the hut before winter, he could at least have built one as Nansen had and survived on what food he had and could shoot.

Wellman thought Andrée might also have come down in the ocean east of Spitsbergen and drowned. Or he might have gone north and east, missed Franz Josef Land, and ended up on the ice. He would then have had perhaps 250 miles to travel across rotten and slushy ice, which would be exhausting.

"In such case the explorers are probably lost," Wellman wrote. "Upon the Polar pack no game can be had, except by the rarest good luck a stray bear comes that way." Even if they had avoided the water, they might in a high wind have been "spilled out or severely injured." Or, given Andrée's having packed his food in the ropes instead of the cab, he and the others might have fallen out and had the balloon sail off without them. If Andrée had made shelter on Franz Josef Land, Wellman thought he would be found alive during the summer of 1899.

48

Andrée began to travel like a shade through the pages of the newspapers. A young Norwegian woman working for a family in Binghamton, New York, said that one night she had awakened to find a figure beside her bed. "At once I knew it as the astral body of Prof. Andrée," she said in the *Washington Post*. Andrée had beckoned to her at her bedside, and she had gone with him over "seas and mountains until suddenly we were upon an open sea, free from ice, into which a point of land jutted. The figure pointed upward, and I saw the pole star was directly overhead." They continued until they came to a tent where "around a fire I saw Andrée and his companions sleeping peacefully."

In January of 1898 the forms of Andrée, Strindberg, and Fraenkel were modeled as waxworks by Madame Tussaud's museum in London. The newspaper in Boston that reported the casting wrote that it amounted to a prediction, since no lost figure cast in wax had ever turned up alive. In March the captain of the Danish steamer *Inga* said he had met the captain of an American ship who had gone ashore in Labrador and found a grave with a cross marked "Andrée." He dug beneath the cross and found a body and a box with some papers. He took the cross with him and showed it to the Danish captain.

The story in the *New York Times* on April 6, 1898, with the headline "Andrée Pigeon in Chicago," that began, "An exhausted pigeon bearing a metal tag inscribed 'No. 23,699, F. Andrée,' was picked up at Forty-Second and Carroll Avenues this morning. A policeman noticed the bird acting strangely, and after some trouble he captured it," was a hoax. So many pigeons had turned up around the world that the *Louisville Courier* ran the headline "A Plague of Pigeons." The story included the sentence, "To the foreigner the impression is conveyed at certain times that the woods are full of pigeons."

By 1899 Franz Josef Land and the area east of Greenland had been searched. The searches were all based more or less on hunches. The area in which Andrée might have disappeared included two hundred thousand square miles—more than California and fewer than Texas, that is.

Beneath the headline "Andrée Bones Found," which appeared in the *Los Angeles Times* in February of 1899, ran a letter, first published in the *Siberian Advertiser,* and written by "a well-known sportsman named La Jalen." The letter said, "I hasten to inform you that Andrée's balloon has been found. I was running in snowshoes after elks in the primeval forest of the South Yenisee and came across traces of Andrée. It was 350 versts (234 miles) from Krasnolars, and 100 versts (67 miles) from the gold washings in Sanvinich, down in the pit of the river. The balloon and ropes were torn and three bodies lay at its side, one with a broken skull. Please prepare assistance so that the balloon and bodies can be brought to the washings at Sanvinich, which can only be done by means of snowshoes. I guarantee the truth of these facts, and shall soon be in Tomsk."

Both Nansen and Nordenskiöld said that they doubted the report. However, the *New York Times* wrote, "There is no reason whatever for distrusting the good faith of the story. There are no yellow journals in North Siberia, and few of any hue, and whatever interest there may have been among the few educated Russians in those parts about the fate of Andrée has long ago lapsed. It is not a rumor-breeding atmosphere." They went on to say, "In any case, there can scarcely now be a doubt that Andrée and his companions have perished, and in any case their fate cannot affect the heroism of their exploit. To push out into space backed only by one's own faith in one's own theory, and to take a chance against overwhelming odds, is the very bravery, for which Columbus has been so honored for these four hundred years. That he found a continent and that poor Andrée has found only a grave makes no difference in the quality of the courage involved."

Nordenskiöld, however, remained confident. In his dining room in Stockholm he had a photograph of Andrée's balloon ascending, and next to it a space where he planned to hang a photograph of Andrée's return—"for I am firmly convinced that he will return," he said.

49

In October men sent to look for Andrée in Alaska were reported by the *Boston Globe* to have given up their search and staked twenty-five gold claims instead. That same month the *Manchester Guardian* printed parts of a letter forwarded to them by "Rear Admiral Campion, C.B.," which he had received from his nephew, "Commander Alston, R.N., who is in charge of Fort Churchill, the most northern trading post of the Hudson's Bay Company, where he had been about five years and talks Esquimaux." In the spring an Eskimo named Stockley had told Alston that the summer before he and his brother had come across a party of white men shooting deer. Some Eskimos approaching them didn't see the deer and thought the white men were shooting at them. Or, another paper wrote, perhaps they objected to the white men, who had arrived in a balloon, hunting on their ground. The *New York Tribune* writer said that the Eskimos, "who are adepts with bow and arrow, immediately discharged a flight of bone darts on their aerial visitors, killing all three." From the balloon the Eskimos took rifles and ammunition and various utensils. In some versions Andrée had arrived in a large white house with ropes hanging from it. In another he had been riding in a bubble that fell from the heavens. When the Eskimos realized that they had killed human beings, they ran away and were unwilling to talk about it. Several of the people who reported hearing the story said that a characteristic of the Eskimos who told it were that they never lied and they never made anything up.

The natives were using the balloon and its ropes to pad their canoes and repair their tents. Since the account had been brought to Winnipeg by a Church of England clergyman, it was for a long time regarded as authentic.

In March of 1900 Nansen said that he had given up hope of seeing Andrée again. "All that can be looked for now," he said, "is the recovery of his body." Even so, in May, one of Andrée's brothers said that he believed that Andrée had probably landed somewhere where it would take him two or three years to reach civilization. The balloon had been "as safe as a railway train," he said. He added, however, that he would give up hope if Andrée hadn't appeared by the end of the summer.

Under the headline "Andrée's Will Made Public," which appeared in the *Atlanta Constitution* in January of 1901, a reporter wrote that the will was accompanied by letters "from prominent scientists encouraging him in the dangerous enterprise," along with one "warning him against it." Andrée had written in pencil on it, "It is possible that he may be right but now it is too late. I have made all my preparations and cannot draw back."

The will contained the sentences, "I write on the eve of a journey full of dangers such as history has yet never been able to show. My presentment tells me that this terrible journey will signify my death."

50

What else? Two of Andrée's sisters, interviewed in Gränna, said that they believed that Andrée went to look for the pole on a mission from God. "And the Lord has never forsaken one of his servants," they said.

The claim that Andrée had been killed by Indians returned in 1910, brought by a missionary. In Chicago a man interviewed at length by a newspaper said that the poles of the earth were entrances to an interior world that was exactly like the outer world and that Andrée had gone over the lip of the boundary and was now at the center of the earth. The man was building a flying machine to rescue him.

Also in 1910 a reporter noted that if the balloon had fallen on the ice or into the water, relics of the sledge or the boat or something stamped with Andrée's brand would have drifted into the path of a ship, as items from the *Jeannette* had.

In 1914 a report that Andrée's balloon had been found in Siberia went round the world. The *Pittsburgh Post* ran a piece that said, "The other alternative is most interesting. He may be away and living in the beautiful region which is said to exist around the pole. If so, he must be in a tropical country, for scientists agree that there is an open Polar sea."

Some people thought that after sending the third message, Andrée had been taken to Greenland by the wind and had come down and hadn't had enough food to make it back. "Starvation would have been their one reward for their sacrifice to science," one writer said. "The probability is that the aeronauts and the records of their achievement will remain fast in their ice sarcophagus for eternity.

"No memorial can be raised above the grave of Andrée and his comrades. And the spot where it should be raised will, perhaps, remain forever unknown."

In a journal Oscar Strindberg wrote his brother a letter he never sent. "When I awake in the morning, and when I fall asleep at night—during walks, at meals, during work, at the theater, constantly I see the image of my beloved son and my fantasy depicts him in various ways; I see him struggling across the unbelievable expanses of ice, drawing his sledge, I see him huddled in a hole built of stone and ice in cold and darkness trying to hold onto the warmth of life, I see him struggling against hunger and hardship, and I see him stretched out and covered in snow, defeated, sleeping the eternal sleep, soiled, tattered and unshaven, but with a calm visage, as if he had fallen asleep knowing that he had done everything humanly possible to save his young life."

51

The experience that Andrée might be having on the ice had been made plain to the American imagination through the case of George Tyson. Few people had as grievous an encounter with the ice fields as he and his party. Tyson was an assistant navigator on the *Polaris* expedition of 1871, which was led by Charles Hall, who was from Cincinnati. Hall had got money from Congress for a voyage to find the pole. This was his third Arctic voyage. Beforehand he had owned a printing business and published a small newspaper. He had also been a blacksmith, and he looked like one. He was about five foot nine inches tall and about two hundred pounds, "muscular rather than stout," Tyson wrote. He had curly brown hair and a thick beard. "Life and vigor seemed inseparable from the thought of him."

Hall liked to read anything he could find about the Arctic. "Everything relating to the arctic zone is deeply interesting to me," he wrote in a journal—"I love the snows, the ices, the icebergs, the fauna, and the flora of the North!" In 1861, when he was thirty-nine, he went there, thinking he would find survivors of Franklin's expedition. To prepare himself he spent a few nights in a tent in Ohio. His urge to go had been a calling, he said. In his journal he wrote, "I am on a mission of love."

Hall was a species of rapturist. Having seen his first iceberg, which he described as "a mountain of alabaster resting calmly on the bosom of the dark blue sea," he wrote, "I stood in the presence of God's work. Its fashioning was that of the Great Architect! He who hath builded *such* monuments, and cast them forth upon the waters of the sea *is God,* and there can be none other!"

The *Polaris* was frozen into the ice off northern Greenland in September of 1871. In October, Hall and a companion left on a sledding trip north and came back in two weeks. Tyson met him as he approached the ship and thought that he looked "very well." Hall, he said, seemed "to have enjoyed his journey amazingly. He said he was going again and that he wanted me to go with him." Aboard the ship, Hall drank a cup of coffee, which he said tasted sweet, and almost immediately he fell sick. In his cabin that evening he told Tyson that he hoped he would be better in the morning.

Instead, Tyson wrote that "Captain Hall is certainly delirious. I don't know what to make of what he says." After several days Hall was out of bed, "but he don't act like himself," Tyson wrote. "He begins a thing and don't finish it." Hall lost feeling on his left side. When his hand was lifted, it fell, and he didn't feel a needle that was stuck in it. The ship's doctor said that he had had a stroke, but Hall told Tyson that he believed someone was trying to poison him.

On November 8 Hall died. Three days later, at eleven-thirty in the morning, he was buried about half a mile from the ship, in a grave that was "necessarily very shallow," Tyson wrote. Despite the hour it was dark, and the stars were out. Tyson held a lantern so that the prayers could be read.

In 1968 Hall's corpse was dug up, and it was determined that he had received large doses of arsenic during the last two weeks of his life. The symptoms of arsenic poisoning are consistent with the ones he suffered. In addition, arsenic tastes sweet. The supposition was that at least three prominent members of Hall's crew—the doctor, the meteorologist, and the sailing master—thought they would die trying to reach the pole, and decided to kill Hall and turn back once the ice freed the ship.

Without Hall the ship's discipline deteriorated. An attempt, which didn't get far, was made to reach the pole. By the fall of 1872 the ship had turned south. In early October it began to leak. By the fifteenth, it was aground on an iceberg. During the night it rose and fell and leaned sideways. The chief engineer, named Schumann, announced that a new leak had sprung. The sailing master, named Budington, gave the order to "throw everything on the ice," Tyson wrote. "Instantly everything was confusion, the men seizing everything indiscriminately and throwing it overboard." While crates and bundles and instruments rained down on them, Tyson and several others stood on the ice trying to keep things from going into the water or landing beneath the ship and being crushed. Tyson went back onboard and discovered that the new leak was a false alarm. When the ship had turned to one side, the water it contained had rushed along with it, and the engineer had supposed a fresh leak. Tyson went back on the ice to try to retrieve the food and equipment.

"Very shortly after, the ice exploded under our feet, and broke in many places, and *the ship broke away in the darkness, and we lost sight of her for a moment,*" Tyson wrote. It was snowing and dark, and the wind was blowing so hard that he couldn't look into it. He didn't know who was on the ice with him, but he knew that there were children because the last thing he had pulled from under the ship, where it might be crushed, was a bundle of ox skins in which two or three children belonging to the expedition's Eskimo hunter had been wrapped. "A slight motion of the ice, and in a moment more they would either have been in the water and drowned in the darkness, or crushed between the ice."

They had begun working at six in the evening, and the ship had broken away at ten. There were men standing on small floes, and Tyson rowed to them in a scow, which got swamped, so he switched to a whaleboat; these were the only boats he had. After everyone was brought together they didn't move much, since in the storm they couldn't tell the extent of the floe they were on. The crew and the women and children huddled in musk-ox skins, while Tyson walked the floe all night. The others had taken all the skins, and he didn't think it was right to disturb them to ask for one.

By the morning the storm had quieted. Tyson scanned the horizon for the *Polaris* and couldn't see it. Why it did not come to rescue them he couldn't understand. He had eighteen people with him—nine crewmen, most of them Germans, and nine Eskimos—the two hunters and their wives and children. The floe was about four miles around, with hills of ice and freshwater pools. Tyson saw a lead that would take them to land, where they might find the *Polaris* or at least Eskimos to help them. He gave orders for the boat to be made ready, but the crew "seemed very inert, and in no hurry." They said they were tired and wet and hungry and needed something to eat before they moved. Tyson knew he could get himself to safety, but if something had happened to the *Polaris* and it couldn't come back, he thought the others would perish, so he waited. After the crew ate, they needed to change clothes. By the time they were ready, the lead was closing and the wind was turning against them, bringing ice with it. They shoved off, but the ice blocked them, and they had to turn back. Soon after, however, Tyson saw the *Polaris* eight or ten miles away, rounding a point of land and "was rejoiced indeed." It was under steam and sail, but through his spyglass he could see no one on the deck. With a piece of India rubber cloth, Tyson set up a distress banner that showed dark against the ice. The *Polaris* did not come toward them but rounded the land and disappeared. "I do not know what to make of this," Tyson wrote.

He sent some men to collect poles from a house he had built for provisions while the ship was moored to the floe. They came back saying the *Polaris* was moored behind the island. From a vantage point and through his spyglass, Tyson saw it with its sails furled.

"I did not feel right about the vessel not coming for us," he wrote. "I began to think she did not mean to." Tyson urged everyone to prepare to make for the island in hopes of reaching the *Polaris*. The men filled the boats with their possessions, which they insisted on bringing. "They seemed to think more of saving their clothes than their lives," Tyson wrote. When they finally reached the water, it turned out they had brought only three oars and no rudder. Tyson set out anyway, in a gale, but with no rudder the wind threw them back against the floe. They were too tired to haul the boat to their camp, so they left it where it was.

During the night the floe separated, and the part with their boat drifted off, along with some of their provisions, and they had to chase after it. Meanwhile the floe they occupied drifted, apparently to the southwest; Tyson couldn't be sure, because he had no instruments. Along with the maps, they were aboard the *Polaris*.

So that there would be no jealousies, they built a small scale and used lead shot to weigh out the increments of food they allowed themselves, "just enough to keep body and soul together," Tyson wrote. Some of the crew were stealing from the storehouse, but the cold was too severe for someone to stand guard. The hunters went out every day after seals but found none. "It is not easy to find seals in the winter," Tyson wrote. "They live principally under the ice, and can only be seen when the ice cracks; an inexperienced person would never catch one." The holes the seals made at the surface to breathe were so small—about two and a half inches across—"that they are not easily distinguished, especially in the dim and uncertain light." Tyson thought also that they were very shy and seemed to know when they were being watched. "A native will sometimes remain watching a seal-hole thirty-six or forty-eight hours before getting a chance to strike, and if the first stroke is not accurate the game is gone forever."

As November wore on there was less to eat. "Some tremble with weakness when they try to walk," Tyson wrote. The Eskimos oversaw the building of a small compound of igloos, connected by passages to one another and to the storehouse. The crew withdrew into their own, in which, although most of them knew English, they spoke German, so Tyson never knew what they were discussing. He prayed a prayer from the Arctic traveler's prayerbook, "May the great and good God have mercy upon us, and send us seals, or I fear we must perish." Wishing they didn't have to, they killed five dogs—they had nine—and ate them. They cut up the smaller boat for fuel. By then they had given up hope that the *Polaris* would rescue them.

Tyson held the highest rank, but the Germans hardly listened to him. "I can scarcely get an order obeyed if I give one," he wrote. To avoid unpleasantness, he tried to do anything that needed to be done by himself. The men stole when they could. They "seize hold of any thing they can lay hands on and secrete it," he wrote. Aboard the *Polaris,* while Tyson was engaged in other matters, each man had been given a gun. Now Tyson was the only man on the floe without one. He shared quarters with one of the Eskimos and his wife and child. These particular Eskimos had been to England and had lived in Connecticut, so he could speak to them.

The hungrier Tyson grew, the colder he got, and the more he thought about food. For Thanksgiving he had two biscuits, dried apples from a can, seal entrails, and some blubber. "I am thankful for what I do get," he wrote. "Thankful that it is no worse." For all but two hours of the day they lived in complete darkness. The rest of the time they had "glimmering light, so that we can just make out to walk over the uneven ice."

As much as he could, Tyson lay still in his hut. "The stiller we keep and the warmer, the less we can live on," he wrote. His clothes were too thin for the cold. Having been working on the floe when the *Polaris* broke away, he hadn't had a chance to get his warmer ones. By December they were living in total darkness, which made it impossible to hunt seals, which they relied on not only for food, but also to burn in their lamps. "Bears only come where seals are to be caught so we need not look for them," Tyson wrote. One of the men shot a scrawny fox, "all hair and tail," and they ate every part of it.

One of the Eskimos, who had two guns, gave Tyson one. "He says he don't like the look out of the men's eyes," Tyson wrote. "Setting aside the crime of cannibalism—for if it is God's will that we should die by starvation, why, let us die like men, not like brutes, tearing each other to pieces—it would be the worst possible policy to kill the poor natives. They are our best, and I may say only, hunters." The Germans swaggered around with their weapons, and conveyed to Tyson the impression that the Eskimos were a burden.

"I see the necessity of being very careful," Tyson wrote, "though I shall protect the natives at any cost." Above all, he thought, a quarrel must be avoided, for "that would be fatal."

Toward the third week of December, Tyson wrote, *"The fear of death has long ago been starved and frozen out of me."*

In January, one of the Eskimos finally killed a seal. Tyson

ordered that it be taken to the Eskimos' hut to be dressed, but the crew took it and "kept an undue proportion for themselves."

Through February they lay in their huts, sometimes bickering. The wind blew continuously. During the first week of March, while they were subsisting on only a few ounces a day— "a well kept dog receives more"—one of the Eskimos shot the largest seal Tyson had ever seen. It weighed between six and seven hundred pounds, and "took all hands to drag him to the huts," he wrote. "It was, indeed, a great deliverance." They had been, he wrote, "just on the verge of absolute destitution." Some of the crew ate until they were sick.

As they drifted farther south, they began to encounter more seals. On a day toward the end of March they shot seven, and on another they shot nine. Bears left their tracks in the camp at night, but the hunters weren't able to shoot any. Meanwhile, the Germans, everlasting tinkerers and mechanical improvers, had dismantled nearly every rifle and most were ruined. "They must work away at every thing, and never stop till it is rendered useless," Tyson wrote.

On the twenty-eighth a bear came into camp and fed on their sealskins and blubber. Tyson, creeping up on it, knocked over a standing shotgun—to prevent their guns from seizing up from the vapors of their breath, they had to leave them outside. When the bear growled, Tyson fired, "but the gun did not go; pulled a second and third time—it did not go; but I did, for the bear now came for me." Tyson made it to his hut and got another shell. He crept out again, saw the bear in the darkness, and as it turned toward him he fired and this time hit the bear in the heart. It ran about thirty feet and fell over dead. The meat, Tyson wrote, tasted "more like pork than anything we have had to eat for a long time."

In a gale at the end of March, Tyson felt "a great thump, as if a hammer a mile wide had hit us," and looked out to see that their floe had gotten in the way of an iceberg. Where they were, he couldn't tell. "Our little ice-craft is plowing its way through the sea without other guide than the Great Being above."

By the first of April their floe had separated itself from the larger one it had been part of and was small enough that Tyson no longer thought it was safe. They decided to use the whaleboat to try to reach the larger floe. They had to leave behind their store of meat, which had grown to a size to feed them for a month, and a good part of their ammunition, because of its weight. What they did bring, in addition to their sleeping gear, was Captain Hall's writing desk. Some of the men wanted to throw it overboard, but Tyson "positively forbade it, as it was all we had belonging to our late commander." Nineteen people, including five children, fit into a boat built for six or seven. The children were frightened and crying. The boat was nearly swamped, but they made twenty miles, spending the night on a floe. They regained the pack on the fourth. Three days later, as they were having breakfast, the floe split beneath their tent. They managed to get out, but their breakfast went in the water. "What little sleep I get is disturbed and unrefreshing," Tyson wrote.

Their boat was so close to the tent that there was no space to walk between them, but the following day, in a storm, the ice split, carrying off the boat, a kayak, and one of the men. "We stood helpless, looking at each other," Tyson wrote. The man on the floe—he was the cook, whose name was Meyers—couldn't manage the boat by himself, nor did he know how to use the kayak. He cast it adrift, hoping it would reach the men on the other floe, who could come get him or at least throw him a line, but it went in another direction. The two hunters went after it, jumping from one piece of ice to another. Night fell. Tyson and the others tried to get some rest. In the morning they could see the boat and the two men, who hadn't the strength to manage it either, and the kayak about a half mile in the opposite direction. Tyson and another man went after them, hopping like goats among the ice. When they reached the boat, all of them were so weak that they couldn't move it. Finally every man in the camp but two, who were afraid to cross the ice, came, and they got the boat back to camp. Along the way two men had to be pulled from the water. "We are all more or less wet," Tyson wrote, "and Meyers badly frozen."

They set up a tent and passed an uncertain night. In the morning the sea was running high—"the water, like a hungry beast, creeps nearer." Tyson wrote. "Things look very bad." That evening the sea overran the tent. They got their possessions into the boat and prepared to launch it, "but I fear she can never live in such a sea." The women and children had begun to spend all their time in the boat, since the ice could split at any moment and they might not have time to reach it otherwise. The sea's overwhelming the floe meant that there was no freshwater ice to melt, and all of them suffered from thirst.

By midnight the ice closed in around them, quieting the sea, and they tried to sleep. In the coming days they saw a fox and some ravens, leading Tyson to conclude that they weren't far from land. They also saw some seals but were unable to reach them. "Are very hungry, and are likely to remain so."

On April 13 Tyson wrote, "I think this must be Easter-Sunday in civilized lands. Surely we have had more than a forty days' fast. May we have a glorious resurrection to peace and safety ere long!" The night before, sitting alone and pondering their circumstances, he had taken hope while watching the northern lights. "The auroras seem to me always like a sudden flashing out of divinity," he wrote. The ice was so close about them that they saw no water and therefore couldn't move. The edges of their floe were wearing away. "Things look very dark, starvation very near," Tyson wrote.

They saw seals but not close enough that they could kill them. Snow fell thickly on the fifteenth, then the sun came out, and although the weather would have been good for traveling they saw nothing but ice around them. "Some of the men have dangerous looks; this hunger is disturbing their brains. I can not but fear that they contemplate crime. After what we have gone through, I hope this company may be preserved from any fatal wrong. We can and we must bear what God sends without crime. This party must not disgrace humanity by cannibalism."

52

On the following day the men's faces were swollen, but Tyson could not tell why. "I know scurvy when I see it, and it is not that." Someone had been stealing from the small store of food they had left, and they had grown so weak that no one could stand watch for more than an hour at a time. A few days later, on the eighteenth, they shot a seal, which gave them enough meat for three meals, although it had to be eaten raw. It happened to be the same day they saw land, which then disappeared in a mist, "as if God had raised the curtain" to keep them from giving up, Tyson wrote.

Meyers, the cook, seemed not to have recovered from his dunking. He wore deerskin gloves that were too large for his hands, so they had no feeling from the cold. He was tall and very thin, and he would bend over and grasp the bones of the seal to try to find one more scrap of meat, "and as he would raise himself up, almost toppling over with weakness, he found time and again that he had grasped *nothing*." Tyson wrote. "If Doré had wanted a model subject to stand for famine, he might have drawn Meyers at this moment and made a success. He was the most wretched-looking object I ever saw."

Around nine that night, the sea overran their tent, while Tyson was in it. Every five or ten minutes a wave washed over them, until one carried away the tent and all their sleeping skins, "leaving us destitute," Tyson wrote. They put the women and children in the whaleboat and dragged it to the edge of the floe where the waves were arriving, and until the morning, they endured "what I should say few, if any, have ever gone through with and lived." A wave would break over them as they held on to the boat and drag them across the floe, sometimes delivering a portion of the boat into the water. Within the waves were blocks of ice as large as dressers, which knocked them down "like so many pins in a bowling alley." When a wave had passed, they dragged the boat back to where they had started, hoping to arrive before another wave hit them. Hardly anyone made a sound, except the children, who were crying, and Tyson who was yelling to everyone to hold on.

When daylight arrived Tyson saw a floe riding peacefully and decided they must reach it. As they launched, the cook went in the water but was pulled aboard. Reaching the floe, they lay down in their wet clothes to rest.

If the sun had come out, their clothes might have dried, but for several days they had snow, sleet, and rain. The exhaustion of the night they had spent hauling the boat settled on them like an illness. They ate some dried skin that had been tanned and was meant for clothing, and was hard to tear with their teeth. They were south of where bears usually hunted, but one appeared and Tyson ordered everyone to lie down on the ice as if they were seals, and when the bear came toward them, the hunters, concealed behind a hummock, dropped it. "We arose with a shout," Tyson wrote. "The dread uncertainty was over."

By the end of April their floe had eroded so much that Tyson was sure it would not survive a gale that appeared to be at hand. Launching the boat, which was now damaged, seemed to be "like putting to sea in a cracked bowl," but they did, and after eight hours of rowing hauled up on another floe. Snow began to fall and did not stop until the next afternoon. The gale set the icebergs moving—"a grand and awful sight"—and they worried about being run over. Then at four-thirty on the afternoon of April 28, they saw a steamer. They hoisted their flag and pulled toward it, but the steamer never saw them, and by the evening it was lost to view. Under a new moon, they hauled up on another floe. With blubber from seals they had just shot, they built a fire, hoping another ship might see it.

In the morning a second steamer appeared, a sealer, and they got in the boat and pulled toward it for an hour, but gave up when the ice closed them in. From another floe, they fired three shots and heard three shots from a steamer several miles away that seemed to be heading toward them through the ice, first in one direction, then another, but getting no nearer. They fired their guns again, but it remained four or five miles away. All day they did whatever they could to draw its attention, without being certain if they were seen. Late in the afternoon it turned away and disappeared.

Through fog on the following afternoon—it was April 30—they saw another sealer, and this time Tyson sent one of the hunters toward it in his kayak. The hunter eventually pulled up beside it and shouted "American steamer," hoping to convey that he came from an American steamer that had been lost. In a few moments the sealer drew up alongside Tyson's floe. A hundred men "covered her top-gallant-mast, forecastle, and forerigging," he wrote. They lowered seal boats, while Tyson and the others threw everything out of their boat to lighten it and got in to row to meet them.

Once aboard, Tyson was pressed with questions. "How long have you been on the ice?" he was asked, and when he answered, since October fifteenth, "they were so astonished that they fairly looked blank with wonder." One of them asked, "And was you on it night and day?"

The *Polaris,* it turned out, had run aground, and the fourteen men aboard had spent the winter in a camp they built with the help of Eskimos who befriended them. Once open water arrived in the spring, they built two boats and set out and were rescued by a Scottish whaler.

Tyson and the others had drifted more than fifteen hundred miles and had arrived off the coast of Newfoundland. When their story was made known, there were Arctic experts who said it was "impossible" and "ridiculous."

53

The *Bratvaag* was hired during the summer of 1930 to take Dr. Horn's geological expedition to Franz Josef Land, with the provision that it would also hunt seals and walruses; the owner wouldn't lease it otherwise. White Island lay in its path, sufficiently secluded that until 1925 its place on the map was east of where it actually is. Over the years the island, which is now called Kvitøya and belongs to Norway, had different names. The first appears to have been Giles Land, sometimes also written "Gillies Land," after a Dutch cartographer named Giles, whose maps describe it as an "ice highland," discovered in 1707. It was called White Island—the name being descriptive of its appearance—in 1876 by a Norwegian sealing captain named Johan Kjeldsen. (In

1887 another captain named it New Iceland, but the name didn't stick.) It was seventeen miles long, eight miles wide, and entirely occupied by a dome of ice that was 660 feet tall.

Horn described the island as "a dazzling white shield seeming to float on the waves from which it rose in precipitous walls of ice." All around it were icebergs, some of them grounded on shoals and reefs. The *Bratvaag's* captain went slowly among them, taking soundings, since the charts gave no depths, and finally anchored half a mile offshore. Horn collected his "geologist's hammers, botanizing boxes, nets, and other scientific equipment," and rode in a launch to shore, passing a herd of walruses. He spent the day hammering at rocks and startling flocks of birds.

The next day, August 6, was "a glittering day, with the sun shining in a cloudless heaven," Horn wrote. "A most intense silence prevailed everywhere, broken only now and then by thunder from the glacier to our north." The walrus hunt began around noon. After a few hours the captain returned to the ship. "He approached us calmly and quietly and told us that they had made a great find. *They had found Andrée.*"

The captain then handed Horn the book. "We were astonished to see how neatly and orderly everything was written," Horn wrote. "It was just as if the notes had been put down in a warm room, and yet the calculations had been made and written during the course of a death-march across the ice."

Ashore, Horn found the sealers gathered around Andrée's boat. "It was strange to stand there and let our gaze wander over the same landscape and the same sea that Andrée and Strindberg and Fraenkel looked at for the last time thirty-three years before," Horn wrote. "It was as if we saw them before us." He pictured them coming toward him, struggling with the boat and their belongings. Seeing the island at last, he thought, must have filled them "with renewed courage, with fresh hopes." He imagined them climbing the glacier to look for other signs of land. "Maybe, one day of clear weather, they caught sight of Great Island's white dome in the west. They knew that behind it lay North-East Land, and behind that again Spitzbergen, whence there was the path home to Sweden."

The camp was beside a sloping rock against which snow had drifted. The boat was on the snow, and one side was covered with it. By the end toward the water were some books, one of which had tables of figures. "Of other objects lying about in the snow we noticed: a square, heavy box which certainly contained ammunition, trousers, a piece of black-and-red cloth, an oblong instrument-box, a barometer; a piece of canvas was found farther off, probably a part of the covering of the boat which had been torn loose by the wind. At about right angles to the boat lay an empty sledge, the upper rail of which was on a level with the surface of the snow, and by the side of which there was found a handkerchief with the monogram N. S. marked with red thread."

Andrée lay about thirty-five feet away. In a pocket inside his jacket was a pencil, a pedometer, and another diary with a few pages of writing. Close by, was the butt of a shotgun whose barrel was in the snow, and a camp stove, which had fuel in it. When they pumped the stove, "the paraffin came out of the burner in a fine spray," meaning it still worked. (In Stockholm it boiled a liter of water in six minutes.) There was also a "china pot of lanoline," a bottle of white tablets, and about sixty yards east a pelvis, which they decided was Andrée's. About forty yards north was "a typical Arctic grave"—stones, that is, piled on a body laid on the ground in the cleft between two rocks. From the stones "feet in their Lapp boots stuck out," and a shoulder. Bears had disturbed the grave; nearby a skull, bleached by the sun, "lay there dreadfully smiling."

Working with mattocks and spades, they began to free the

boat from the ice, then discovered that it was lashed to a sledge underneath it. They were too heavy to lift, so the men cut the boat free and began to excavate the sledge.

For a while they stood beside Andrée, wondering if it was proper to move him. They decided that he should be brought home, along with whoever was buried beneath the stones. Having removed them, they discovered that the body was frozen to the ground and had to be hewed free, which was difficult because the cleft was so narrow that they could work only from the ends.

Others among the crew piled stones on a ridge above where Andrée had lain. Inside the cairn they placed a bottle containing a note that described their having found "the relics of the Swedish Andrée Expedition," and so that the cairn could be seen from the water they put up a white pole steadied by three guy wires.

On a tarpaulin they carried the bodies to the shore, then went back for the boat, which was filled with ice and so heavy that when they placed it aboard a whaleboat, the whaleboat sank nearly to its gunwales. Towing it to the ship by a motorboat took an hour. "Later on, Ole Myklebust made a chest, rather more than two yards long, with two compartments," Horn wrote. "The skeletons were placed in the larger compartment—Andrée with the gun by his side—while in the other were put all the smaller objects that had been found beside Andrée."

The next day they left, watching White Island disappear in fog.

54

The following day, August 8, the *Bratvaag* met the *Ternigen*, a sealer from Tromsø, Norway. When they told the captain what was in the box on the foredeck, the news "made a great impression on him, for everyone knew Andrée," Horn wrote. "He had become, so to say, a legend." The *Bratvaag* had no radio with which they could send messages—they could only receive them—so they asked the *Ternigen,* which was heading home, to convey word of their find. They planned to be gone some time on Franz Josef Land.

As it happened, they stayed a little more than two weeks. Coming home, they passed White Island. Through a telescope they saw the pole by the cairn, and a bear walking on the beach. The sea was running too high to allow them to land and see if they could find anything more. On the evening of the thirtieth one of the crew appeared on deck saying he had just heard a message calling them home. They all ran down into the hold and heard it broadcast again.

The following morning, hoping to trade bear meat for fish, they met a fishing boat, and were told that a lot of vessels were looking for them. They put into Hasvik, on Sor Island, to make telephone calls and send telegrams "and so for the first time came into contact with a world that seemed to be a trifle excited," Horn wrote. They stopped next at Skjaervo, where the *Fram* had stopped, and found journalists everywhere. They were ordered to sail to Tromsø, to meet an escort and the commission appointed by the government to receive the remains.

55

In Tromsø a black pall was brought from the cathedral and laid over the box that held Andrée and, it turned out, Strindberg.

Sealers from the *Bratvaag*—"a group of young men with weather-beaten faces, bare-headed," the account in *The Andrée Diaries* says—carried the box to a hearse that was drawn by a horse. Along with relatives of Andrée and Strindberg, the crew walked beside it, leading a procession the mile to the hospital. Once the remains had been laid on tables in the sick ward, it was seen that Andrée and Strindberg were wearing the clothes they had left in. In Andrée's pockets was a little black leather purse that had in it objects that had belonged to Strindberg. Among these was a gold heart with a photograph of Anna Charlier, and a lock of her hair. There were also two chronometers—one belonging to Strindberg, and one attached by a gold chain to a locket with photographs of Andrée's mother and father, and to a gold ring with two garnets and a piece of turquoise. Around Andrée's waist was a blue wool jersey. The doctors who opened it found some sennegrass and within the grass, a book with writing in pencil from cover to cover.

After the doctors finished, Andrée and Strindberg were placed inside zinc coffins embedded in oak caskets, which had been brought from Sweden, and the caskets were draped with the Swedish flag. It happened to be Thursday, September 4, Strindberg's birthday. Monday evening, at the cathedral, the coffins were arrayed side by side at an altar. "Tongues of fire from innumerable lights quivered around the altar, which was adorned with a wealth of flowers," the report says. Andrée's and Strindberg's relations sat on each side of the nave. For the people who couldn't fit in the cathedral, speakers were hung on the houses around it, "where multitudes stood listening with the greatest attention." The sermon drew on the verse from Revelation that begins, "And the sea gave up the dead which were in it."

The preacher went on to observe, according to the report, that "many had said that it was a 'madman's journey' to travel over the ice northwards in a balloon. It was possible that these men had been urged by some slight touch of human vanity, but innermost there lay an ideal craving to explore a world. They were the first who had endeavoured to penetrate the regions of the Arctic by the air. Others had succeeded them with better results, but if no one had ventured to take the first, dangerous step, these later results would never have been obtained. Sweden may be proud of having owned these men who had not quailed before their task."

56

A number of journalists had gone looking for the *Bratvaag.* Some went to ports where they thought the ship might put in, and some chartered boats to find it at sea. Among these was the *Isbjorn,* an old, battered Norwegian sealer with its pilothouse aft. The reporters aboard, when they couldn't find the *Bratvaag,* decided to go to White Island. By the time they arrived, in early September, more of the ice and snow had melted.

On the first day a journalist named Kurt Stubbendorf found bones that turned out to belong to Andrée. Presumably when the *Bratvaag* had been there, they were under snow. The following day, Stubbendorf wrote, "an iron bar, which we were using against the side of the rock to reach what we took to be some thawed-out rags of reindeer skin, struck against something with an arresting sound." He got down on hands and knees and pressed his face against the ice and saw "the head and upper body of a man lying on his left side, his left arm bent upwards, with the hand beneath the head.

"The dead man was frozen fast to the ground, and I gained

the impression that he had lain undisturbed, embedded in the ice deep below the surface, ever since death had touched him."

Freeing him from the ice, and pulling aside several layers of clothing they saw "K.F." stitched on an undershirt.

Fraenkel's remains were taken to Tromsø, to join those of Andrée and Strindberg. On the fifteenth, the *Svenskund,* which had delivered the expedition to Dane's Island in 1897, retrieved them and their artifacts and brought them to Sweden.

57

Early in the afternoon of October 5, 1930, escorted by five destroyers and five airplanes, the *Svenskund* reached Stockholm. As it approached the harbor, more and more boats fell in behind it until there were nearly two hundred in its wake. While the bells in all the churches tolled, the coffins were carried onto a pier built to receive them and laid in the rain at the feet of King Gustav V, who said, "In the name of the Swedish nation I here greet the dust of the polar explorers who, more than three decades ago, left their native land to find an answer to questions of unparalleled difficulty."

Each coffin was placed in an open car to ride to the cathedral. A funeral salute of ten guns was fired. Standing at the pulpit, the archbishop said, "Welcome home, Andrée! Welcome home, Strindberg! Welcome home, Fraenkel!"

That evening a memorial was held in the City Hall. The secretary of the Swedish Academy, E. A. Karlfeldt, gave a talk, "Andrée and National Feeling." The coffins remained in state for a few more days; then on October 9, Andrée, Strindberg, and Fraenkel were consigned to the flames.

58

The *Isbjørn* had been able to stay at White Island only three days before the concern over being caught among drifting ice led it to leave. The last thing the journalists found was a pair of snow-shoes. Among the artifacts recovered were some notebooks and a few tins of film. Stubbendorf began drying the notebooks in his cabin. "I have seldom, if ever, experienced a more dramatic, a more touching succession of events," he wrote, "than when I began the preparation of the wet leaves, thin as silk, and watched how the writing or drawing, at first invisible, gradually became discernible as the material dried, giving me a whole, connected description written by the dead—a description which displayed unexpected and amazing details, and which allowed me to follow the journey of the balloon across the ice during the three short days from July 11 to 14, 1897."

Each man had kept an account. Fraenkel's was composed of terse, meteorological observations. Strindberg had made astro-nomical observations and records of their meals, in addition, now and then, to notes regarding the journey, and for a while he had written letters to Anna Charlier in shorthand, presumably so the others couldn't read them. The two diaries that belonged to Andrée are the most complete and the most descriptive.

The first night was wonderful, Andrée wrote, while Strind-berg and Fraenkel slept. He was cold, but he didn't want to wake them. Earlier the three of them had drunk some ale then spliced some of the ballast lines to the guide ropes. After Andrée went to lie down, Strindberg and Fraenkel "converse in a whisper," Strindberg wrote. "Everything is silent and quiet." Clouds kept them from seeing the ice, so they couldn't be sure what direction they were heading. When the clouds broke Strindberg determined it was north. "We are now traveling horizontally so beautifully that it is a pity that we are obliged to breathe as that makes the balloon lighter," he wrote. For a time he made observations that Fraenkel wrote down.

Andrée came back on watch at two in the morning on the twelfth, around the time that the balloon began drifting west. At five he heard an auk, which looks a little like a penguin but can fly, and saw a fulmar, which looks like a gull. "The snow on the ice a light, dirty yellow across great expanses," he wrote. "The fur of the polar bear has the same colour." Perhaps because he was looking down on the ice, its contours escaped him. It appeared to be flat, "no signs of hummocks. A horse and sledge could drive over it if the surface is hard." He saw no land. "It is indeed a wonderful journey through the night." The ingenuous tone of his remarks might be accounted for by the three of them being the first men to see the ice fields from the sky.

At six they took a photograph of a seal, which may have been a walrus. They saw two of them, one of which "grew frightened," Andrée wrote, "the other not." Under clouds the balloon descended to fifty feet. Around seven it stopped and didn't move for forty minutes, then it began heading west with the wind. They made breakfast at eight, the coffee taking eighteen minutes to boil. "Pleasant feeling prevails," Strindberg wrote.

For most of the morning they traveled through mist. The temperature was just warmer than freezing. A little after eleven they released four pigeons. One tried to land in the balloon net, then circled the balloon and flew off. Two landed on the ice and disappeared in the fog. Early in the afternoon Strindberg noted, "Blood-red ice perhaps a relic of a bear's meal." Minutes later the balloon sank so low that twice it struck the ice. They threw out the heavy knives they had used to cut the ropes at the launch, a small iron anchor, and fifty-five pounds of sand. The balloon went forward at about five miles an hour, but it didn't rise. They threw out the large buoy they had meant to jettison over the pole. It is difficult to know what the gesture meant. None of the three men was much like the self-revealing and declatory Nansen. Where he wrote set pieces about the sky, the way the ice looked and sounded and its geometry, and what he was thinking, Andrée and the others made brief remarks about bearings and temperatures. It is reasonable to assume that shedding the polar buoy signified an awareness that they weren't going to reach the pole, let alone North America or Russia or Asia—that by the end of the first whole day they were already defeated in their intention, though not in their resolve. It is also possible, however, that the buoy was closest to hand in a crisis and went over when one of them reached for something and didn't pause to consider what it was. Or that, regardless of their intentions, it weighed what they needed to lose and nothing else did. Or that, being essentially an ornament, it was more easily given up than food or medicine or tools or scientific instruments. Their notes are dutiful and pointed and don't include judgments. No one wrote anything more than that it had been shed. Perhaps from familiarity, perhaps from superstition, Strindberg only called it the big buoy.

The balloon not only didn't rise, it underwent "continuous bumps against the ground," Strindberg wrote. It traveled a little more than eight feet per second. Fog kept it close to the ice. If they shed enough weight to make it rise above the mists, the gas would warm in the sun and the balloon would rise higher, losing gas. Having lost gas, they would sink until they were back where they had been, but with less gas and fewer things to discard.

During the next few hours the balloon struck the surface continually—"8 touches in 30m," "bumpings every fifth minute," and "paid visits to the surface and stamped it about every 50 metres"—nevertheless, "humour good," Andrée wrote.

That night one of the drag ropes caught beneath a block of ice and held fast. Alone on watch, Andrée wrote that having thrown out so much ballast during the day, he was content to stand still rather than ascend and find a current that might possibly take them to Greenland. Because of "the repeated bumpings" no one had slept, "and we probably could not have stood it any longer," so he sent Strindberg and Fraenkel to rest at around eleven-thirty. He hoped to let them sleep until six or seven, if he could manage to stay awake.

"It is not a little strange to be floating here above the Polar Sea," he went on. "To be the first to have floated here in a balloon. How soon, I wonder, shall we have successors? Shall we be thought mad or will our example be followed? I cannot deny that all three of us are dominated by a feeling of pride. We think we can well face death having done what we have done. Isn't it all, perhaps, the expression of an extremely strong sense of individuality which cannot bear the thought of living and dying like a man in the ranks, forgotten by coming generations? Is this ambition?"

All night Andrée saw "not a living thing," no "bird, seal, walrus, or bear." The only sounds were "the rattling of the guide lines in the snow, the flapping of the sails," and the whining of the wind as it worked through the basket. Strindberg got up around six. The fog thinned, and here and there were patches of blue sky. Strindberg wondered "if there will be a high-level flight." He woke Fraenkel around nine-thirty. Around eleven, the balloon lurched forward and the cab struck the ice and they broke free, after thirteen hours. Strangely, if the rope had not held them, the wind that blew through the night would likely have carried them back to Spitsbergen.

Around noon they had a meal: châteaubriand, the king's special ale, chocolate with biscuits and raspberry syrup, and water. Strindberg said it was invigorating. Afterward he sat in the bearing ring, where the concussions were softer, and it was "confoundedly pleasant. One feels so safe there and so at home." He made an inventory of his outfit. "Clothing in which I am dressed July 13, 1897 is: one Jaeger-wool jersey, wool hunting shirt, a pair of wool pants, a Blue 'army suit,' a wool-lined leather waistcoat, a pair of rather thin woolen stockings, one cap (woolen), a pair of fur-lined snowboots, a pair of woolen mittens." Meanwhile Andrée tried to sleep in the basket, "but I expect he will not get any proper rest," because it continued to strike the ground intermittently.

Fog covered the sun again, and a light rain settled as hoarfrost on the ropes. On the ice they saw bear tracks. They sent off another four pigeons. One flew away, then returned and "circled a few times in the neighborhood of the balloon." Among these was the bird that landed in the rigging of the *Alkern* and was shot.

The balloon sank low enough that the basket was more or less being dragged over the ice. They threw out a medicine chest and a buoy, but rose only slightly. To Andrée the ice looked smooth enough to travel on, but he was concerned about crossing the leads. "No bird is seen or heard, and so I suppose there is no land near," he wrote. Then he said, "I received a hard blow on the head," but from what is illegible. The next entry suggested that he was pleased that the balloon had not lost much gas.

59

That evening the concussions against the ice made Strindberg seasick. They shed six small buoys, a winch, 165 pounds of sand, a barrel, and a few other things amounting to 440 pounds, and the balloon rose sufficiently that Andrée was able to set the sails. "They carry excellently and increase the speed. The balloon goes extremely beautifully. Altogether it is quite stately."

Meanwhile Strindberg sat in the bearing ring with Fraenkel and read Anna Charlier's last letter again. "It was a really enjoyable moment," he wrote.

That night Andrée noted that "an immense polar bear" swam a hundred feet below them. "He got out of the way of the guide-lines and went off at a jog-trot when he got up on the ice." Through the fog the horizon looked "bewilderingly like land. It has deceived me several times." What ice he could see looked "easily traversed if there were no water on and between the floes."

Fraenkel went to bed around nine, then Andrée and Strindberg shot the sun—used a sextant, that is, to determine its position and fix their latitude. At ten-thirty the basket struck the ice hard several times. Around midnight the longest of the guide-lines broke. They were enveloped in a deep and constant fog. "No land and no birds, seals or walruses," Andrée wrote. One of the pigeons returned and flew around the balloon. "Perhaps it has done the same as Glaisher's pigeon?"

Andrée meant James Glaisher, an Englishman, from Wolverhampton, who had made the highest ascent in a balloon in 1862, when he rode to thirty-six thousand feet. At twenty thousand feet "I laid my arm upon the table possessed of all its vigour, and on being desirous of using it I found it powerless," he wrote. "I tried to move the other arm and found it powerless also." As he looked at the barometer "my head fell on my left shoulder." He managed to raise it, but then it fell on his right shoulder. Glaisher had gone aloft with a partner named Coxwell, who was up in the ring, making an adjustment, and Glaisher tried to speak to him but "an intense black darkness came, the optic nerve finally losing power suddenly." He came to hearing Coxwell say, "Do try—now do." He rose as if from sleep and said, "I have been insensible," and Coxwell said, "You have, and I, too, very nearly." Coxwell's hands had turned black, and Glaisher poured brandy over them, possibly to warm them.

Glaisher had taken six pigeons aloft. One was set free at three miles and flew off; one was released at four and flew away but "taking a dip each time; a third was tossed out between four and five miles and fell downward like a stone." A fourth, thrown out on the descent at four miles, flew in a circle and landed on top of the balloon. The other two were brought to the ground. One was dead and the other, a carrier, "would not leave the hand when I attempted to throw it off." Finally it left and flew to Wolverhampton and was "the only pigeon that has been heard of."

Andrée "adjusted the steering apparatus at its maximum southwards"—it was around two-thirty in the morning—and set a course to the north. About forty-five minutes later he cut the side sails loose. At six-twenty "the balloon rose to a great height," but he opened the valves and immediately brought it back close to the ice.

"Anchored on an ice-floe 7:30 a.m., July 14," Strindberg wrote. The flight was all but done. About forty minutes later they jumped out of the basket, "worn out and famished," according to Andrée.

They had made the longest flight ever, having been aloft for sixty-five hours and thirty-three minutes, had traveled 517 miles, and were about 300 miles north of where they started, approximately 300 miles from the pole.

60

Andrée landed the balloon so expertly that none of the birds was injured and not even the most sensitive of their instruments was damaged. It lay on its side—the huge orb, flattened like a tire against the ice. The rigging and the ropes enclosing it made it appear as if it were a live thing that had been pursued and brought down. Andrée and Fraenkel stood looking at it, as if the first to arrive at the scene of a disaster or a remarkable anomaly, while Strindberg walked off on the ice and took photographs of it.

The next morning Andrée wrote that the balloon had been heavily encumbered by ice from the fine rain and the fog. (By now it was only a flat piece of dark fabric; trash beside the basket.)

All around them were ice and ruins of ice, pieces heaved up and toppled and ground into angles and corners like sawteeth. Here and there were leads and pools of water resembling ponds

and channels. From the air the leads had looked like deep open water, but now they saw that some were only shallow streams formed by melted ice.

They had left as explorers, and now they were adventurers. Explorers study accounts of trips similar to their own as closely as scholars study an absorbing text. No concern is too slight to entertain. In *A Thousand Days in the Arctic*, Frederick Jackson, the man who met up with Nansen, described an explorer about to leave on a sledging trip who was observed in his cabin weighing a handkerchief and trying to decide if he could bring it. Adventure arrives on a voyage of discovery in the form of a mistake, and is almost always unwelcome. It is as if an explorer had conceived a plan for a trial voyage and then carried it out the way a scientist conducts an experiment. Roald Amundsen, who was first to the South Pole, in 1911, said that people often thought of adventure when they encountered the word discovery. A voyage of discovery was "a race against time, in order to escape death by starvation," he wrote. An adventure was "an error in his calculations, the fact of which the 'experiment' has exposed."

It took them a week to build their boat and choose what to

pack in their sledges. Meanwhile there were periods of snow and rain. On the morning of the twentieth the pigeons flew away, and that evening Andrée shot a bear that came close to the camp. Strindberg cooked it, and they ate it with "excellent pumpernickel." The next day they tried the boat in a lead with "extremely good result."

They might have stayed where they were and let the ice carry them, as Tyson had, but no science could be done on an ice floe, or any new territory seen. In addition, to drift to rescue was passive and symbolically meager, whereas polar exploration was confrontational. Ernest Shackleton, the British explorer, called polar work "the white warfare," after trying to traverse Antarctica in 1914. "Twice I examined the horizon carefully in every direction without discovering land," Andrée wrote. He was about 192 miles from North-East Land, part of the Spitsbergen archipelago, and about 210 miles from Franz Josef Land, where Nansen had spent the winter. No one had ever crossed the wilderness between him and either place; he hoped to find land and shelter that was closer and unknown.

61

On the evening of July 22, they began walking southeast toward the depot that Jackson had left for them on Franz Josef Land. Their sledges weighed between 300 and 450 pounds. Strindberg noted that they were very hard to pull. Two hundred and fifty pounds had been the weight that had led Nansen's crewman to conclude that "if a man had to draw a load like that he might just as well lie down at once—it would come to the same thing in the end."

At midnight they camped, and Strindberg wrote Charlier, "Well, now your Nils knows what it is to walk on the Polar ice. We had a little mishap at the start. When we were crossing from our ice-floe with the first sledge it went crooked and fell in. It was with difficulty we succeeded in getting it up. I climbed down up to the knees and held fast the sledge so that it should not sink. Andrée and Fraenkel crossed over to the other ice-floe and then suddenly we managed to get the sledge up but I expect that my sack which was on the sledge is wet inside. And it is there that I have all your letters and your portrait. Yes, they will be my dearest treasure during the winter. Well, my dear, what will you be thinking all winter? That is my only anxiety.—Well, after we had got the sledge up again we piloted ourselves across some floes with channels of water between. The way we did it was by making the ice-floes move quickly so that they came near each other. This was slow work with the large floes of course. At last we came on to a large field of ice across which we travelled with our sledges two or three kilometers. Each is loaded with about 160 kg. so

that they are very heavy and during the last hour what we did was for all three of us to help with one sledge at a time. Now we have encamped on a picturesque bit of ice and have pitched our tent. In the tent we have our sleeping-sack in which all three of us are now lying side by side. It is a squeeze but the fellowship is good. Well, there is much I should write about but now I must sleep. Good night."

When they woke at eleven-thirty in the morning, the sun was among clouds. To make breakfast and pack the sledges took an hour and they started walking around one. The leads were hard to cross and Strindberg and Andrée had different ideas about how to, although neither wrote them down. Andrée wrote, "The traveling bad and we were extremely fatigued. Dangerous ferry-ings and violent twistings, etc. of the sledges among the hummocks." They discussed whether to lighten the sledges but reached no conclusion. It was Charlier's birthday, and they gave her four cheers.

"We have just stopped for the day," Strindberg wrote her, "after drudging and pulling the sledges for ten hours. I am really rather tired but must first chat a little. First and foremost I must congratulate you, for this is your birthday. Oh, how I wish I could tell you now that I am in excellent health and that you need not fear for us at all. We are sure to come home by and by."

What Strindberg wrote next has faded away. When the text began again, he said, "Yes, how very much all this occupies my thoughts during the day, for I have plenty of time to think and it is so good to have such pleasant memories and such happy prospects for the future as I have, to think about!

"*(Later.)* Now we have camped for the night and had coffee and eaten our sandwiches with cheese and h . . . biscuits and syrup and . . . Just now we are putting up the tent and Fraenkel is taking the meteorological observations. Now we are enjoying a caramel, it is a real luxury. You can fancy we are not over-delicate here. Yesterday evening I gave them (for it is I who attend to the housekeeping) a soup which was really not good, for that Rousseau meat-powder has a bad taste one soon becomes tired of it. But we managed to eat it in any case. . . .

"Well, we have stopped for the night on an open place, round about there is ice, ice in every direction. You saw from Nansen's pictures how such ice looks. Hummocks, walls, and fissures in the sea alternating with melted ice, everlastingly the same. For the moment it is snowing a little but it is calm at least and not especially cold (–0.8°). At home I think you have nicer summer weather."

Strindberg's tone then turned downcast. "Yes, it is strange to think that not even for your next birthday will it be possible for us to be at home. And perhaps we shall have to winter here for another year more. We do not know yet. We are now moving onwards so slowly that perhaps we shall not reach Cape Flora this winter, but, like Nansen, will have to pass the winter in an earth-cellar. Poor little Anna, in what despair you will be if we should not come home next autumn. And you can imagine how I am tortured by the thought of it, too, not for my own sake, for now I do not mind if I have hardships as long as I can come home at last.

"Now the tent is in order and we are going to our berths. We are all rather tired but in good humour. We discuss our mental characteristics and our faults, a very educative . . . I chat with . . ."

They awoke on the twenty-fifth to rain and stayed in their tent, sleeping, until three. "Then we rose and I cooked a little food—cocoa and condensed milk and biscuits and sandwiches," Strindberg wrote Charlier. "At 4.30 o'cl. we started and now we have drudged and pulled our heavy sledges for four and a half hours. The weather is pretty bad: wet snow and fog, but we are in good humour. We have kept up a really pleasant conversation the whole day. Andrée has talked about his life, how he entered the Patent Office, etc. Fraenkel and Andrée have gone ahead on a reconnoitering tour. I stayed with the sledges and now I am sitting writing to you. Yes, now you are having evening at home and you, like I, have had a very jolly and pleasant day. Here one day passes like another. Pulling and drudging at the sledges, eating and sleeping. The most delightful hour of the day is when one has gone to bed and allows one's thoughts to fly back to better and happier times. But the immediate object now is our winter-place. We hope to find things better in the future. Now the others are coming back and we shall continue the drudgery with the sledges, Au revoir. . . ."

Strindberg did not tell Charlier that he had fallen into water deep enough that he "was in imminent danger of drowning," Andrée wrote. After being rescued, he was "dried and wrung out and dressed in knickerbockers."

That evening Andrée made a list of all the items he carried on his sledge, which weighed 459 pounds. It included a shovel, three bamboo poles, a hose, a tarpaulin, a boat hook, and one "basket with contents," which on its own weighed 143 pounds. Strindberg calculated that in pulling one sledge and returning for another, they had made perhaps a mile and no more than two in the last five days. They decided to shed what they could so that each man's sledge weighed little enough that he could pull it himself. What they would do is take sufficient provisions and equipment to last forty-five days. Andrée got his sledge down to 285 pounds, and Fraenkel got his to three hundred. "Strange feelings and great indulgence in food on making reduction," Andrée wrote.

That day Strindberg shot a bear, his first. They soaked it for an hour in salt water which made it, according to Andrée, "immensely good." The wind, having blown from the north, swung around to the south, which Andrée hoped would make the ice drift with them as they walked.

On the twenty-seventh, to lighten the sledges again, they got rid of some meat powder and bread, which they thought they wouldn't need, since Fraenkel had also shot a bear. They had tried to frighten it off by blowing a whistle and a hunting horn, then Fraenkel had "put in a beautiful shot at 38 m.," Andrée wrote. With the skin they patched their sleeping sack.

Most of the day they spent crossing leads, one while rowing, two others pushing the boat across. The leads had ice in them that was difficult to move, and cut the boat. The day was "extremely fatiguing," Andrée wrote, so that even Fraenkel said he was tired.

In the tent the next day, they drank a bottle of champagne, possibly the one they had brought to celebrate crossing the pole, and ate some biscuits with honey. The day was easier than many. They saw bear tracks but no bears. "Now we have turned in 12 o'cl. noon the 29th after having thus been at work 16 hours," Andrée wrote. "We learn the poor man's art: to make use of *everything*. We also learn the art of living from one day to the next." Then he made a note to "Describe in detail. Difficulties with the ice, the ice-humps, melted snow-water, the sludge pools and the leads and the floes of broken ice."

On the thirtieth Fraenkel had incipient snow blindness but didn't take any treatment. Their camp tasks had fallen into a pattern. Strindberg boiled and fried, serving bear meat twice a day, and Fraenkel took meteorological notes, oiled the guns, made sandwiches, and set the table and cleared it. "I reconnoiter," Andrée wrote. At meals they sat on a medicine chest, a piece of photographic equipment, and a case of matches. To protect his hands from drying and cracking Andrée smeared them with bear grease.

"Now it is a long time since I chatted with you," Strindberg wrote Charlier on the thirty-first. The brief letter, roughly five sentences long—because parts have faded it is not possible to be certain—describes their changing the loads on their sledges a few days earlier. It was a letter Strindberg didn't finish, and it was the last he wrote to her. After that he wrote only in his diary. It is an indication, perhaps, that he felt less hopeful.

They took astronomical measurements and discovered that the ice had drifted west faster than they had walked east. "This is not encouraging," Andrée wrote. "Out on the ice one cannot at all notice that it is in movement."

62

On the morning of the thirty-first, they got under way at four. A fog kept them from seeing the best route. The snow was deep, and repeatedly they sank to their knees; Strindberg fell often, "flopping," Andrée called it. When they came to an immense field of pressure ice—ice heaved up by collisions, that is—they had to cut their way through it. "The Polar dist. is certainly the source of the idea of the stumbling block," Andrée wrote. He climbed a large pyramid-shaped piece of ice, but could see no land or water, even though, while resting earlier, they had heard "a murmuring noise as from a sea."

Toward evening they crossed bear tracks. "He had gone down in the soup a couple of times so hard that not even he is above making mistakes in this regard," Andrée wrote.

They saw the back of an animal they hadn't seen before, "which looked like a long snake 10–12 metre long," Andrée wrote—about thirty-three to thirty-nine feet—"of a dirty yellow color and, in my opinion, with black stripes running from the back for some distance down the sides." He heard it breathing heavily and supposed it was a whale.

The day was not difficult but when Andrée woke up more tired than usual the next morning, he wrote, "It seems as if good country were more fatiguing than half-good."

They began to run out of food. "The last bear meat was cut into small pieces so that it might at least look like being a lot." An hour after breaking camp, however, Andrée shot a bear in the chest at 125 feet, "an old worn-out male animal with rotten teeth." Strindberg and Fraenkel had shot at it too ("both fired outers"). Andrée hoped that the remains would draw other bears "so that we shall always have fresh meat at our heels." From heavy wire Andrée made a fork for Fraenkel because the bear meat was so tough that it bent the forks they had. Strindberg stood the fork against a box in the boat and took a photograph of it.

In ten hours they made a little more than a mile. Cutting a path, they destroyed their ax. When they came to a challenging place to cross, one of them would say, "Is it easy to get across?" and another would answer, "Yes, it is easy with difficulty."

On August 4 they gave up walking east. "We can surmount neither the current, nor the ice," Andrée wrote. They decided to start southwest, toward a smaller depot on the Seven Islands, which they hoped they might reach in six or seven weeks. The temperature dropped to about twenty-eight degrees. "Each degree makes us creep deeper down into the sleeping sack." The cold froze leads inconsistently, which left the three of them sometimes having to cross uncertain ice on hands and knees. When they ran low on bear meat, they ate mainly bread, biscuits, and water. In "extremely clear air" Andrée searched with a spyglass for land or water and saw none. "Only ice and very difficult ice visible in all directions," he wrote.

Between August 4 and 6 they were at nearly the same place they had been in the balloon between one-thirty in the morning and three on July 12.

63

In the *Proceedings of the Royal Geographical Society* for August of 1875, Adm. Sir Francis Leopold McClintock published a piece with the title "On Arctic Sledge Travelling," in which he wrote that the first sledge party to look for Franklin had managed five hundred miles in forty days. They had two sleds, each drawn by six men. "The labour of doing so is most excessive," he wrote, and of the twelve men at the end "five were completely knocked up, and every man required a considerable time under medical care to recruit his strength."

People unacquainted with sledging tended, he wrote, to think "that we either skate over glassy ice, or walk on snow-shoes over snow of any considerable depth," he went on. "Salt-water ice is not so smooth as to be slippery; to skate upon it is very possible, though very fatiguing. But hardly is the sea frozen over, when the snow falls, and remains upon it all winter. When it first falls, snow is often soft, and perhaps a foot or fifteen inches deep; but it is blown about by every wind, until having become like the finest sand, and hardened under a severe temperature, it consolidates into a covering of a few inches' depth, and becomes so compact, that the sledge-runner does not sink more than an inch or so: its specific gravity is then about half that of water.

"This expanse of snow is rarely smooth: it is broken into ridges or furrows by every strong wind." These "inequalities are seldom more than a foot high, they add greatly to the labour of travelling, especially when obliged to cross them at right angles.

"As the spring season advances, the old winter snow becomes softened, fresh snow falls, and sledging is made more laborious still.

"At length the thaw arrives; the snow becomes a sludgy mixture, with wet snow on top and water beneath, through which men and sledges sink down to the ice below. It is now almost impossible to get along at all."

Moreover, "We seldom find either unbroken ice, or ice so crushed up into ridges that we cannot get over it at all, but, as a rule, crushed up or hummocky ice, three or four feet in height, is of very frequent occurrence, and of course adds much to the labour of sledging."

Sir George Nares, who led an expedition to discover the pole in 1875, tried to prepare his crew for sledging by telling them "that if they could ever imagine the hardest work they had ever been called upon to perform in their lives intensified to the utmost degree, it would only be as child's play in comparison with the work they would have to perform whilst sledging."

Typically while sledging, men ate six or eight pounds of meat a day and sometimes as many as sixteen.

64

Turning toward the Seven Islands on the fourth, they crossed uneven ice. "Often the most practicable crossings lie at the ugliest hummock," Andrée wrote, because the leads were narrower there. They walked for six hours, had a meal of biscuits, butter, and cheese, then walked six hours more. When they left their tent to start again, it was raining.

By the sixth they had arrived at a level plain extending about a hundred yards, but which was covered with "powdered-sugar ice and ice gravel," against which they slipped and fought for their footing, Andrée wrote. Crossing a lead, the sledges rolled several times, which led Fraenkel to say that the journey could not be called altogether hopeless—a pun from the Swedish word that emphasized hop. The wind was against them and seemed to drive them back as far as they advanced. "New difficulty: the leads altering while we are crossing them," Andrée wrote.

Bear meat was "very good when it has become old," he continued, and a little reindeer-hair in the food, from the sleeping sack, was recommended, "for while taking it out one is prevented from eating too quickly and greedily." The wind was "right in our noses, but it is cooling." In the brightest light he needed dark glasses. The rest of the time he squinted.

When they came to "a dreadful country" with pools of fresh water, Fraenkel, who was in the habit of complaining of the monotony of the landscape, "did not like what was offered him," Andrée wrote. Freshwater pools, more than saltwater ones, were usually too shallow to cross in the boat and their edges tended to be smooth and slippery.

9 Aug. at 2:20 a.m. we began to get up in the tent
3:00 the primus started
3:18 the steak ready and the coffee-making begun
3:29 the steak eaten
3:48 the coffee made
4:00 the coffee drunk
5:30 broke camp

The terrain they faced consisted "of ice-humps blocks and hills with snow-drifts between and this is difficult for the pullers," Andrée wrote. Fraenkel began to suffer from the runs, and Andrée gave him opium for it. In addition, he grew despondent. A bear approached but turned tail before they could shoot it, though Strindberg and Fraenkel chased it. "This was a great grief for us and a pity too for soon we shall have no more bear's meat left." The next problem was Strindberg's gun, which was poorly made, and had to be fixed. By the time they got into their sleeping sack, they had been up and working for eighteen hours.

Andrée's sledge still weighed nearly 300 pounds, and he made another inventory of it: one gun, one box of ammunition, a tent, a medicine chest, two tent poles, five pounds of meat, and various instruments and private items. Fraenkel carried the boat, which weighed nearly 139 pounds, the oars, some books, a gun, ammunition, hay for their shoes, eight boxes of matches—altogether 338 pounds.

The ground they crossed next Andrée described as "absolutely untrafficable"—broad channels with clumps of ice and snow through which neither the boat nor the sledges could pass except laboriously. By Strindberg's calculations they had passed south of eighty-two degrees longitude, and to celebrate they had sardines for dinner, at four in the afternoon, with bread, biscuits, butter, and cheese. Fraenkel's stomach was better. Afterward it began to rain, and in the evening to snow. They walked until ten that night.

Late in the morning—it was August 11—Andrée and his sledge went into the water, soaking everything aboard. Strindberg's sledge ran into Fraenkel's, and a grapnel it was carrying poked a hole in the boat. Each of their sledges rolled several times. Twice Andrée's landed upside down. "All imaginable difficulties happened and when the evening came we were not at all happy," he wrote.

"Something else happened," he added. "F. shot an ivory gull." He described the gull's markings and feet. "The beak had a yel-

low point but was otherwise yellowish-white with black longitudinal shadings. The bird landed quite near us."

For the first time they changed course to reach what they thought was land but discovered was only a peculiarly shaped piece of ice. A parallel line of narrative in Andrée's diary is the observations he made now and then on natural history—on the consistency of the snow or the elements such as clay that he sometimes found among the ice, and what they suggested about where the ice had originated. In their specificity his notes have a suggestion of mania. "Sample no. 7 was found near the edge of a melt-hole and on the *under*-side of a thin, newly formed ice covering about 2cm thick lying over the water in the same melt hole."

From readings they thought they were close to Gillies Land—that is, White Island—"but neither that nor any other land is visible," Andrée wrote. Having only one meal of bear left, they fried a gull and liked how it tasted. Before going to bed, at three-thirty on the morning of the thirteenth, they heard a whale and looked for it but didn't find it.

Later that day they tried to catch a seal and failed. In a fissure, with a shovel, Andrée killed a small fish, probably a polar cod, by his description, which "seemed astonished to see us." Almost at the same moment Strindberg yelled, "Three bears!" They hid behind a hummock, but no bears appeared. Softly whistling, Andrée crept forward as bait, then lay down in the snow. The she-bear left her cubs and came toward him but scented him and retreated. Andrée lay still in the snow, hoping she might return, and when he could stand it no longer he yelled that they should rush the bear. The bear came toward him, they fired but missed, and Andrée leaped up, wounding the bear as she fled. With his next shot he dropped her, and with the fourth he dropped one of the cubs. Fraenkel wounded the other, and Strindberg dropped it. From them they got 138 pounds of meat, sufficient for twenty-three days. The heart, brain, and kidneys they had come to like especially, as well as the tongue. With butchering the bear, they didn't walk much that day. The following day they ate themselves "prop full," Andrée wrote. He noted that the mother bear had bitten her tongue clean through, then he wrote, "The ivory gull has three cries 1. piyrrrr with four soft and trilling r's 2. pyot-pyot 3. resembling the croaking of the crow."

The next day it rained. They stayed in their tent and mended their glasses and sharpened their knives. Andrée said they ate "masses of meat." He and Strindberg both had the runs, and Strindberg cut his hand. They left in a snowfall at four in the morning and made good progress through terrain that Andrée wrote was "very bad."

On the seventeenth Andrée wrote, "Our journey today has been terrible. We have not advanced 1000 meters but with the greatest difficulty have dodged on from floe to floe." On the eighteenth, from open water between floes, seals watched them get in and out of their boat time and again, trying to ferry their way through troublesome ice. "We must be near the sea, the ice being so divided," Andrée wrote. It was a clear day, and they could see the horizon distinctly, but no land appeared where they hoped it would be. All their effort had again taken them not much more than a thousand yards.

Mending his pants later in the tent, Andrée heard a noise and, looking through a crack, "saw a bear close to my nose." Still sewing he said, "Look, there's another bear for us." Fraenkel crept out of the tent and as the bear rose to attack him he shot it. It turned out to be a young male, the best of all the bears they had shot, and from the brain, the kidneys, the tongue, and some steaks along the back, they got twenty-two pounds of meat.

With some of it, Strindberg baited fishhooks, which he dropped through the ice, but he didn't catch anything.

Snow concealed irregularities in the ice, which slowed the sledges, and detouring around pools too shallow for their boat meant that they couldn't travel in a straight line. To find a path Andrée would walk ahead. "I have to go a long way among hummocks and over pools and along the leads," he wrote. "The worst are the fresh-water pools which turn in innumerable windings, real labyrinths, and which are united by means of wide fissures that do not become visible until one is close to them." Meanwhile Strindberg and Fraenkel sat shivering with the sledges.

The hidden contours of the ice led frequently to what Andrée called "wild crossings," in which the sledges turned over or hung above "an abyss while the puller tumbles down." Over certain kinds of ice the sledges had to be hauled as fast as the three of them could manage and over others inch by inch, or rotated at speed on a pivot point. When their way was blocked they would cut a track with an ax or a spade. Other terrain required that they unload the sledges completely. To cross deeper leads they had to balance the sledges between the gunwales of the boat, which left them always in danger of tipping over. Even a small lead, if it was only half frozen or filled with ice, might take hours to cross cautiously.

One evening toward the end of August, Andrée proposed that they try bear meat raw, which, if you salted it, tasted like oysters, he wrote. It was the twenty-first, and while they were pitching their tent three bears came at them. Strindberg shot one, and Fraenkel shot the other two. At Andrée's suggestion Fraenkel mixed some of the bears' blood with oatmeal and fried it in butter, which they called a blood pancake and thought was excellent. Strindberg then put algae and yeast powder together for a soup which Andrée wrote "should be considered as a fairly important discovery for travelers in these tracts."

Early in the morning Andrée shot a young ivory gull. "It seems to be one of the young ones that give the cry 'pyot-pyot,' " he wrote. The *piyrrr* call he had decided was the mother's call of concern. He preserved its eyes so that they could be examined for how they were defended against snow blindness. The country the three of them faced consisted of "a boundless field of large and small hummocks. One cannot speak of any regularity among them," he wrote. Just as they crossed a lead it closed. "The floes came at a great speed and there was a creaking sound about us. It made a strange and magnificent impression." The day, he said, had been "perhaps the most beautiful we have had." With the horizon's being so clear they tried again to sight land, with no luck.

They had grown fatigued but were undaunted. Andrée could still find beauty in where he found himself. Of the formations of ice on a peaceful clear night he wrote, "Magnificent Venetian landscape with canals between lofty hummock edges on both sides, water-square with ice fountain and stairs down to the canals. Divine."

The same day, August 22, Fraenkel's knee was dislocated but

went back into its joint without difficulty. His foot was sore, and Andrée massaged it. Strindberg had pain in one of his toes.

The next day a lead opened just where they about to cross, and they had to stop and ferry the boat over instead. Fraenkel made a soup with algae and bear meat, which Andrée liked but Strindberg and Fraenkel thought should be only an "emergency soup." The temperature had fallen so that the ice in the pools had begun to support their weight, meaning that they wouldn't have to travel such curving courses. With all the bears they had shot, they were now each eating six pounds of meat a day, and thriving.

About eight inches beneath the surface of a lead, a small, dark gray fish, perhaps four inches long, glided among the pieces of ice. They saw it only briefly. "Fulmars and ivory gulls sail around us pretty often," Andrée wrote. A small black bird "with white on the wings like a black guillemot, but white under the belly like a little auk," they were unable to identify. "It has a kind of twitter and we have not seen it fly but only dive." To preserve a sample of leaves and clay ("Find no. 17"), Andrée washed it in a tea-strainer, then wrapped it and dried it against his chest.

Fraenkel had developed a severe case of the runs, which Andrée thought came from his having caught cold. Also he suffered "sometimes from cramp perhaps on account of overexertion." Strindberg's toe had been cured by rubbing boot grease on his sock, which probably reduced the abrasion.

Andrée saw a bird, which he thought was a skua, a gull-like bird, that flew "as silently as a spirit." He also saw the sea-serpent-like animal again, which was "gray everywhere and when he dived a two-cloven fin was seen."

Later in the day—it was August 25—Fraenkel fell in the water. He still had the runs, and Andrée got them too. One of Strindberg's feet also had begun to hurt. That evening Andrée made six fishhooks from pins, strung them nineteen inches apart, baited them with bear meat and fat, and set them sixteen feet beneath the ice. He left them for two days, but nothing touched them.

On the twenty-seventh, they had one of their best days, making roughly four miles in very good weather. Fraenkel was still suffering from the runs, and Andrée gave him opium for it. Andrée's case seemed to have gotten better without his taking anything.

Andrée put out his fishing line again, but still nothing touched it. They broke camp at nine and walked across ice that "was very much in movement," he wrote. By midday they had reached "terrible ice: large hummocks with deep perpendicular pools between." In the evening Fraenkel had pain in his stomach, and Andrée gave him morphine. "We shall see if he can be made a sound man again."

The gulls and the fulmars came so close that Andrée was tempted to kill them with a stick. They discovered that the movement of the ice had thwarted them again, and that in six days they had come only twelve miles. "To keep a tolerably steady course among the leads is on my word no easy task."

The next day, August 29, Andrée wrote that he had started to feel the cold. The floor of the tent had begun to be covered in ice. A bear they wished they could shoot ran "off at a gallop when he saw that he was noticed." The ice had turned hard as glass and was difficult to pull a sledge across.

"Tonight was the first time I thought of all the lovely things at home," Andrée wrote.

65

On the thirtieth they started walking at five in the evening, with the temperature at twenty degrees. When they arrived on a floe they couldn't leave except in their boat, they decided to pitch their tent and see if the floe moved during the night. A bear crept up until it was about ten feet from Strindberg, who finally saw it and shouted. Andrée was inside the tent, but Fraenkel was outside and wounded it. To save cartridges they let it run for a while, although it took three more shots to kill it, and it ended up in a lead where they had to use the grapnel and a rope to collect it. Strindberg took a photograph of it lying on the ice, with Andrée and Fraenkel standing beside it. From it they got meat to last fourteen days.

The following day they again began walking in the evening. "The sun touched the horizon at midnight," Andrée wrote. "The landscape on fire. The snow a sea of fire." The polar summer was finished. Not a soul in the world knew where they were.

They came to a sheet of new ice, which Andrée crept across on hands and knees. Then they passed among ice that was moving. "It is fine to work the sledges onward through the middle of the crashing ice-pressures round about us," Andrée wrote. "Sometimes a lead closes just when we need it, sometimes it opens suddenly the moment before or after a crossing."

That night Andrée had the runs—from having gotten a chill, he thought—and took both morphine and opium. The next morning, September 1, he wrote that "we needed to be out of harness for a day." They mended the sleeping sack and "chatted and ate and drank. We were in the best of humours." They resolved to try and keep day-and-night schedules.

On the third they rowed for three hours "slowly over the mirror-like surface," as if already in the afterlife. "We knew that we were moving onwards more quickly than usual and at every turn of the leads we asked ourselves in silence if we might not possibly journey on in this glorious way to the end," Andrée wrote. They came to a bay full of ice that closed as they arrived, so they had to get out of the boat and return to hauling their sledges.

The fourth was Strindberg's birthday. Andrée woke him and gave him letters Charlier and his family had written for the occasion, which pleased him immensely. In his honor they allowed themselves extra food for dinner—bear's meat, goose-liver paste, and cake with syrup—and they made speeches. Not long after they started traveling, Strindberg fell in the water, soaking him so thoroughly that they had to pitch their tent to dry him out. His sledge, which carried their bread, had gone in with him. They dried the bread and fried what they could, but there was nothing to do with the sugar except pour the water it had dissolved in into their coffee. "It was a pretty great misfortune for us," Andrée wrote. "On such a journey as this there is developed a sense of both the great and of the little. The great nature and the little food and other details."

From tracks they could tell that a bear had come close to them in the night. Twelve ivory gulls settled on a piece of ice beside the tent, and Fraenkel killed three with one shot. After four hours' marching, they got in the boat to cross a lead and ended up rowing through the following night, then pitched their tent on a floe. When they woke, the openings around them had frozen, and only with great effort did they reach the next floe. From the top of it they saw a better route, and along it they saw a walrus, which Andrée realized had been the sea serpent. Walruses sometimes swim in single file, cutting the water like dolphins, and Andrée had apparently seen a line of them and thought from a distance they were one long creature. They took to the boat again but were forced from it by sludge that was formed by pieces of new ice piled on top of one another "like tiles or cards in a pack," until the pieces formed a mass they couldn't penetrate.

After five hours of walking on the following day, the seventh, they had gone a thousand yards. Low on meat, they shot two gulls. "We do not like to shoot unless we can get at least two gulls per shot," Andrée wrote. "They are delicate birds but I think they cost a lot of ammunition." He wished for a seal or a bear.

Neither Fraenkel nor Andrée had the runs anymore, but Fraenkel had pain in his left foot from a blister that Andrée tended. He hoped it would heal soon, since they depended on Fraenkel's strength. On the ninth, Fraenkel could not pull his sled any longer, only push it. Andrée and Strindberg hauled theirs, then returned for his. "This tries our strength," Andrée wrote. Since the terrain had been very difficult, they could manage only six hours' walking. Andrée came to a piece of ice that seemed stable when he tested it with the boat hook but turned out to be sludge, and he fell in. He floated on his back until the others could extend an oar to him. He finished the day's entry by noting that large seals swam around them, but they could not shoot well enough to kill them instantly, and if they only wounded them the seals sank.

66

"Since I wrote last in my diary much has changed, in truth," Andrée wrote ten days later—it was the seventeenth of September. Snow had fallen, making sledging harder. Fraenkel's foot was no better, and Strindberg and Andrée were still pulling his sledge.

One of Strindberg's feet had also begun to hurt. In addition they were nearly out of meat. The current and the wind carried them persistently "down into the jaws between North-East Land and Franz Joseph Land," Andrée wrote. Pinned down by the wind on the eleventh and twelfth, they concluded that they had no chance of reaching the depot on North-East Land. Between August 4 and September 9 the ice had carried them eighty-one miles south-southeast, instead of southwest as they had intended. Spending the winter on the ice had become unavoidable. "Our position is not specially good," Andrée wrote.

Wintering in the Arctic, and especially on the ice, was nothing anyone other than Nansen had ever wanted to do. Horrifying things happened, and the best that could come of it, everyone knew, was that you might still be alive in the spring, although likely diminished. The approach of a winter in the ice led the venerated sledger McClintock to write, "The dreaded reality of wintering in the pack is gradually forcing itself upon my mind,— but I must not write on this subject, it is bad enough to brood over it unceasingly."

The first people to overwinter were those who had their ships frozen in place. Among these was a ship commanded by Willem Barents, the Dutch navigator, which got stuck in 1596. Barents was making his third Arctic voyage, on which he discovered Spitsbergen. At the end of August, in a harbor called Ice Haven, the ship was caught and violently bound, and the crew realized, as one of them wrote, that they would have "in great cold, poverty, misery, and grief to stay all that winter." From driftwood, since no trees grew on the land, they built a house, which took a month. Often they had to quit work to run away from bears. The house was so cold that the fire hardly warmed them. They put their feet in the fire so that their socks burned. They knew to withdraw their feet because they smelled the wool burning, not because they felt the heat.

67

Andrée decided to cross in the boat to another floe, bigger and "richer in ice-humps" than their own, which was "low and small and full of saltwater pools." Theirs, they thought, would break up in the spring. On the new floe they hollowed out a big piece of ice, then built walls from blocks of ice and snow over which they threw water to harden them. Andrée shot a seal through its head, so it didn't sink. Over the following three weeks they ate all but the skin and bones. Bears seemed to have disappeared from the territory, and all they had of animal life were the gulls, which Andrée said were "not to be despised" but cost a lot of ammunition. "May we shoot some score of seals so that we can save ourselves," he wrote.

Fraenkel's foot had gotten a little better but was weeks from being healed. Strindberg's feet were now bad, too. "Our humour is pretty good," Andrée wrote, "although joking and smiling are not of ordinary occurrence. My young comrades hold out better than I had ventured to hope." Andrée thought that perhaps they might drift far enough south that they could get food from the ocean. Also, closer to the water might not be as cold as on the land. "He who lives will see," he wrote. "Now it is time to work."

On the nineteenth, "for the first time since 11 July," Andrée wrote, they sighted land. He was sure it was New Iceland— White Island—and he made a drawing of its long, low outline, rising and sloping from one edge to the other like the curve of an eye. He guessed it was about six miles away.

Going ashore appeared to be impossible, since the "entire island seems to be one single block of ice with a glacier border," Andrée wrote. On the west and east, however, it might be reached. Seeing land meant that the ice had moved so rapidly beneath them that Andrée wrote, "If we drift in this way some weeks more perhaps we may save ourselves on one of the islands east of Spitsbergen."

The following day, the eighteenth, Jubilee Day in Sweden—the twenty-fifth anniversary of King Oscar II's reign—Andrée shot a seal. Cutting it up, he discovered that the skull was "as thin as egg-shell," and should therefore easily be killed by a shot to the head. They hoisted the Swedish flag, drank to the king's health, and sang the national anthem. Strindberg wrote down the menu:

BANQUET, 18 SEPT. '97
ON AN ICE-FLOE IMMEDIATELY EAST OF

Seal-steak and ivory gull fried in butter and seal-blubber, seal-liver,—brain, and kidneys.

Butter and Schumacher-bread.

Wine.

Chocolate with Mellin's-food flour with Albert biscuits and butter.

Gateau aux raisin.

Raspberry syrup sauce.

Port wine 1834 Antonio de Ferrara given by the King.

Toast by Andrée for the King with royal Hurrah:

The national anthem in unison.

Biscuits, butter, cheese.

A glass of wine.

Festive feeling.

During the day the union-flag waved above the camp.

"The general feeling was one of the greatest pleasure and we lay down satisfied and contented," Andrée wrote.

68

The following day Andrée shot two seals. "I cannot describe how glad I felt and how pleased my comrades seemed to be and how they looked forward to the future with hopes considerably strengthened," he wrote. White Island had "the appearance of being transparent," and they took photographs of it. On the following day they shot a bear, which had come swimming toward them through water that was so thick with ice that when they retreived the carcass they had to use a shovel to part the ice. With the new bear they had food to last until April—through the winter, that is. In fact they had so much meat that it became a problem to protect it from bears in the night. They piled it by the edge of the tent and built a fence around it with whatever they found at hand.

Mixing snow and freshwater to make walls and allowing them to freeze, Strindberg—"the architect," as Andrée described

him—began building a house where they could spend the winter. Meanwhile, discord of some kind had begun to surface among them, although Andrée did not say what it was. He said only that the completion of the house was becoming important. "During the last two days the weather has been very pleasant but on the other hand they have not passed without signs of differences arising between us." He hoped these would not fester.

During the night of the twenty-second they heard the floe break, as if underneath them. They thought they might have run aground, but the bearings they took showed that they were moving, perhaps in a backwater created by the island.

The three of them began working on the house, "cementing together ice blocks," Andrée wrote. Above the walls Strindberg was making a vaulted roof. They would get up and work for two and a half hours, then have breakfast, then work until 4:45, altogether eight hours, after which they would have lunch and dinner in one meal.

On the twenty-eighth, although the house wasn't finished, they moved into it, and christened it "Home." To protect their meat from the bears they brought it inside with them.

By the twenty-ninth they were still off the south side of the island. The sludge ice had frozen solid, and the seals had left, but there were still plenty of bears. "The night-bears seem to be a kind of thief bears," Andrée wrote. "The one that visited us yesterday night dragged away our big seal twice and we should have lost it if S. had not succeeded in coming so near the bear as to frighten him." Meanwhile their floe had grown smaller—its edge came close to their hut. The temperature was about seventeen degrees.

The evening of the first of October "was as divinely beautiful as one could wish," Andrée wrote. The water struck him as being "alive with small animals"—they watched gulls swimming, and seals. They expected to finish the house the following day, but that isn't what happened. Instead, at five-thirty in the morning there was a crash, and water began streaming in. They ran out and saw that their floe had split into smaller ones. One of the cracks had opened so close beside them that a wall of the house hung from the roof with nothing below it but water. Their floe was now only about eighty feet around. "This was a great reversal in our position and our prospects," Andrée wrote. Their possessions, among them two bear carcasses with meat for three or four months, floated on different pieces of ice, and they had to race to collect them. "No one lost courage," Andrée wrote. "With such comrades, one should be able to manage under, I may say, any circumstances."

Strindberg wrote tersely in his diary, "Exciting situation."

Worn out from collecting their belongings, they spent the night in the house, even though it was dangerous to do so. Andrée did not seem eager to move ashore. Maybe he felt that the ice would carry them far enough south that they would meet a sealing boat or a whaler, whereas if they spent the winter on land they could not possibly hope to meet anyone until the winter was over.

In any case they stayed on the floe and started another house. On the fourth, having moved with the pack, they could see a lowland on the island where there was no ice, "a refuge if we don't drift too far past," Andrée wrote. What they needed was somewhere to land their belongings. One they had seen earlier they could no longer reach. Andrée thought they would have to move from one small floe to another till they got to one large enough to serve as a platform from which they might see how to approach the land. "This afternoon five birds were seen flying toward the island," Andrée wrote. "They were probably eider-ducks or geese."

They went ashore finally on the fifth, landing on the glacier, then making their way to the land they had seen. Carrying their possessions took them until late at night and, since they were tired and had difficulty lighting their stove, they ate cold food in darkness under the northern lights, "which neither lighted up nor warmed our camp," Andrée wrote. By the time they got into their sleeping bags it was the next day, which was Wilhelmina Andrée's birthday, therefore Andrée called the camp and its vicinity "Mina Andrée's Place."

When they woke it was snowing, and the wind was piling the snow in drifts, so there wasn't much work they could do. They made a small tour. Some distance inland they found driftwood. In the evening they began a snow house on a different site. Andrée decided that their first camp was too vulnerable to being buried by drifting snow.

To determine where they were, they climbed the glacier, which was higher than it had appeared from the sea. In the afternoon they saw a bear coming in from the ice, but when it saw them it turned away. The birds plagued them, especially the gulls trying to steal their meat. "They fight, scream, and struggle," Andrée wrote. "In their jealousy they no longer give the impression of innocent white doves, but of being outright beasts of prey."

Despite the weather's keeping them in the tent for nearly all of the eighth, they collected enough driftwood to lay the beams for their house. "It feels fine to sleep here on fast land as a contrast with the drifting ice out upon the ocean where we constantly heard the cracking, grinding, and din."

Andrée concluded his last entry, "We shall have to gather driftwood and bones of whales"—for the house—"and will have to do some moving."

The bones and the driftwood were collected; the house was never built.

69

Explorers kept diaries mainly to publish them. Even when they accepted that they weren't going to return, they often wrote in the hope of the diaries' being found and having their last thoughts known. Like the notes of some suicides, explorers' diaries sometimes followed their subject to the moment he lost consciousness. Andrée's last entry might have been only a prelude to a gap in his attentions. He might have felt that he needed to establish a shelter and that he would write when he had, the way Nansen interrupted his narrative. After all, there was little else to do but write while waiting for the winter to pass. Or something may have happened to weaken him or make him despair and give up.

When they died isn't known, but they probably didn't last much longer. The evidence of their provisions and belongings remaining in the boat suggests that they had never really established their camp. There was also the driftwood that had been gathered in a pile but not used. Strindberg's diary has a final notation, for October 17, "Home 7:05 a.m.," but it is made in ink, whereas all the other entries are in pencil. Ink freezes. A persuasive explanation offered by scholars is that Strindberg made the notation before they left, expecting to arrive home in Stockholm by train at 7:05 in the morning.

What killed them isn't known either, or even if they died from the same cause. People thought lead poisoning from the metal cans might have done it. Or an accidental gunshot wound. A drowning after a fall through the ice while chasing a bear or looking for driftwood. Dehydration. A psychotic episode of murder. Suicide using opium. Scurvy, or trichinosis, or vitamin A poisoning from polar bear livers, which are rich in it, or maybe botulism. A polar bear attack, or asphyxiation caused by fumes from a cookstove in a tent that was covered with snow and therefore unventilated.

Murder and suicide are unlikely, since their spirits appeared to have held to the end. On none of their clothes were any bullet holes found, nor did the skulls have any. Andrée's gun was beside him, and his back was against a wall, so it isn't plausible that a polar bear crept up on him. Strindberg's vest and shirt had tears on one shoulder, suggesting a polar bear attack, but the tears were more likely caused by the bear that separated his skull from his corpse. They knew about the danger of eating polar bear liver and avoided it. In the late 1990s, a fingernail was found in one of their mittens and tested for lead, and it turned out to have a lot of it, but not a sufficient amount to kill someone. Three months isn't long enough to die from scurvy, and they would have recognized its symptoms, prominent among which are bleeding gums, sunken eyes, and severe fatigue. Also the fresh meat they ate should have been sufficient to protect them. Trichinosis, which is common in polar bears, is not likely, either, because the diaries mention none of the symptoms of a severe infection—muscle pain and fatigue especially. (The runs are a symptom of its onset, but theirs disappeared once they began eating bear fat.) Asphyxiation doesn't seem probable, because Andrée had wrapped his first diary in sennegrass and placed it at his back, against the rock, a gesture that he would likely have been unable to make if he had lapsed abruptly into unconsciousness. Furthermore it is not entirely certain that Andrée and Fraenkel were both within the boundaries of the tent. Botulism is prevalent in Arctic seals and might have killed them if they hadn't been able to cook their food properly, and there is a question of whether the bacteria responsible for it can prosper in such cold.

Perhaps they simply wore themselves out dragging three- and four-hundred-pound sledges on long days through the Arctic for nearly four months while often not having enough to eat. The sailors from the *Bratvaag*, seeing the woolen jerseys and cloth coats that the three men were wearing, decided that they had died of cold and exhaustion.

A peripheral mystery is the order of their deaths. It is generally assumed that Strindberg died first. His being the only one buried supports this notion, but Andrée felt responsible to Strindberg's family for bringing him home safely. It may be that Fraenkel, to whom Andrée felt no special obligation, died first and that Andrée and Strindberg might have been planning to bury him when Strindberg died and Andrée had the strength only to bury him. Or Andrée might have died before having a chance to bury Fraenkel. Something about the shared nature of Andrée and Fraenkel's deaths, however, their being found in similar postures of resignation, as if they had awaited their ends, and close to each other, suggests that the assumption that Strindberg died first is true.

Their ashes were buried in Stockholm on October 9, 1930. For years Gurli Linder had kept a flower in a vase by Andrée's photograph. "Then you came to Stockholm," she wrote. "The King himself was there to hold a speech of welcome. I attended with Greta and Signe"—her sisters—"It was strange. I did not actually feel anything. It was as if it was not you, as if it did not concern me. All that happened since became unreal and irrelevant."

Andrée had kept Linder's letters in a box. Atop them he placed a note, meant to be read when the box was opened. "Thanks my dear for all the happiness you have given," he wrote. "Forgive me for all the pain you have got. Forget me, but not totally! Farewell! Farewell! Your truly devoted."

Linder wrote, "I can still feel the pain I felt when you said, 'You or the expedition—it must come first.'"

70

Who finally discovered the pole is disputed. Frederick Cook, an American, said he reached it on sledges, with two Inuits, in 1908, but he couldn't prove it. Another American, named Robert Peary, said that he got there in 1909, but among his party, which included a black man from Maryland named Matthew Henson and four Inuit, he was the only one who could read navigational instruments. Also, as he closed on the pole, his sleds, according to his diary, went faster and faster, sometimes twice as fast as they had gone earlier in the approach. In addition Peary described traveling a straight path to the pole, whereas Henson said they had had to make detours around hummocks and leads. The first sighting of the pole no one quarrels with was made in 1926, when Roald Amundsen, who had been first to the South Pole, fifteen years earlier, flew over the North Pole in an airship, seeing it from exactly the vantage that would have been Andrée's.

Oscar Strindberg died in 1905, not long after he had begun writing a book about Nils, in which he described him as his favorite son.

Nils Eckholm died in 1923. Early in the twentieth century he became known for expanding the ideas of Svante Arrhenius, Strindberg's physics teacher, and predicting that more carbon dioxide in the atmosphere from burning coal would "undoubtedly cause a very obvious rise of the mean temperature of the earth." Rather than be harmful, though, this circumstance would enable human beings to "regulate the future climate of the Earth," Eckholm wrote, and prevent the arrival of the ice age that had been predicted by a respected Scottish scientist named James Croll.

Fridtjof Nansen died in May of 1930, a few months before Andrée was found on White Island. After his Arctic trip he became a statesman. Toward the end of his life he worked at the League of Nations, overseeing refugee rights, and in 1922 he won the Nobel Peace Prize.

Adolphus Greely died in 1935. He retired from the army as a major general. There is a Greely Island in the Franz Josef Archipelago, which is now part of Russia, and a U.S. postage stamp, issued in 1986, which shows him with a full beard, more or less as he looked several days after he was rescued. So far as I can tell, no journalist sought him out to ask what he thought of Andrée's being found. Enough years had passed that perhaps no one recalled his opposition to Andrée's plan.

Anna Charlier died in 1949, having never reconciled herself to Strindberg's disappearance and death. She had periods of illness and poor health and was in and out of hospitals and sanitariums. She once wrote of herself that she was "ill in body and soul." Now and then she lived with Strindberg's family. Oscar Strindberg wrote of her in 1900, "There are times when she is mourning, but she never torments anyone with her pain and despair." Having watched her shaken by each episode of news about Andrée—by that time simply reports of a buoy being found, or a story emerging from the frontier—he wrote, "Her faith is cruel and hurts my heart . . . I cannot believe how brutal life sometimes can be."

In 1901 Charlier lived in Switzerland, where she worked for a clockmaker, handling Swedish correspondence. Late in the year she went back to Stockholm and became godmother to Sven's son, Ake. She continued to study piano and perform but had to stop frequently from illness. For a time she worked as a housekeeper.

After thirteen years Charlier married a saintly Englishman named Gilbert Hawtrey, who taught French at St. Paul's School, in New Hampshire. At St. Paul's she gave music classes, and on Saturday nights led a music club that met at her house. The students would discuss a different composer each week and sometimes play one of his works. Then they would have a meal characteristic of the country the composer was from. For Verdi they ate spaghetti, and for Wagner they had sauerkraut. A reminiscence in the school's archives describes her as being "old and tottering but known in youth for her beauty. As a pianist, she had played in all the great concert halls of Europe." In a window in the living room of the Hawtrey house was a stuffed pigeon with its wings spread.

On September 4, 1949, which would have been Strindberg's seventy-seventh birthday, a few people gathered at his grave in Stockholm. Tore Strindberg held a small silver box, conveyed by Gilbert Hawtrey at his wife's request.

"Anna could never forget her heart's first love," Tore said. "For her it stood as something sacred. And something broke within her during the latter years of her life—perhaps due to grief.

"When her worried life came to an end—and we remember with sadness the joyous dream of her youth, her musicality, in which her lively and warm intellect perhaps most clearly shone and through which a strong bond with Nils grew forth."

The case was inscribed:

Ashes from near the heart of Anna Albertina Constancia Hawtrey
    (nee Charlier)
    to be placed near the grave of Nils Strindberg
    to whom she was engaged in 1897
    —and may the Great Conductor allow them both to share in
the
    Music of the Spheres.

"May peace be with her," Tore said.

71

One winter I went with a friend to their grave, which occupies a hillside in a small park in Northern Cemetery. Pine trees enclose the grave on three sides. At the top of the hill is a monument, about twelve feet tall, designed by Tore. It is in the shape of a sail, set into layers of stone that approximate the prow of a ship cutting the water. Engraved on the sail is the route of their flight and the walk on the ice.

It has become fashionable in recent years, as attitudes have changed, to regard Andrée as willing to lead younger companions to their deaths if that was the price of fame and accomplishment. This theory is based on the belief, which isn't easily supported, that Andrée knew that he couldn't succeed and was too weak a figure to face the embarrassment, with all the world watching, of either calling off the expedition or sailing over the horizon and landing. Andrée was in early middle age, whereas Strindberg and Fraenkel were young. Fraenkel was not given to introspection—his journal entries were purely scientific—and he was chosen to be the packhorse. Strindberg's nature was less hardy; he wept at leaving Stockholm and Charlier. Andrée was the resolute figure, and they must have trusted that he would see them through. Especially at this remove, he is an aloof, somewhat stern, even monumental figure. Someone who conducts a large degree of his life in his mind, someone not easily influenced or reasoned with. An enigma. He may have been a type more common to the nineteenth century, when fatal, visionary deeds were more frequently enacted on a grand scale, when such behavior was seated within a tradition of valor, commerce, and scientific inquiry. His purposes were deeply serious, and in none of his writing does the idea that he wanted to be famous for the sake of being famous ever appear, or that he regarded fame as something that would stabilize an insecure personality, or even that he had any vanity, other than the wish to have his example validated, to see balloons carry passengers and freight around the world and to places that couldn't be reached by any other means.

Certainly there was a romantic element to his thinking, but if he was self-deluded or calculating, he agreed to suffer for it. The tone of his journals is of a man who believes that discipline and character can overcome formidable obstacles and that such efforts are what great accomplishments require.

An Andrée scholar named Urban Wrakberg defended Andrée in a paper called "Andrée's Folly: Time for Reappraisal?" published by the Swedish Royal Academy of Sciences in 1999. "The widespread notion that Andrée was an aspiring sensationalist and, intellectually, an isolated dreamer out of touch with the real polar science and technology of his period is distressingly close to the complete opposite of the reality," Wrakberg wrote.

I think this is true, with qualifications. It takes nothing from Andrée's courage or daring to observe that while planning his voyage he seemed susceptible to self-persuasion. Fog and shadows caused problems for balloons, but the Arctic was as big as Europe, he said, and just as Europe was not permanently fogbound, the Arctic was not either. Then clouds and fog forced his balloon to the ice. Once he landed he was a man with a desk job trying to cross a landscape as punishing and inhospitable as any in the world. Fraenkel and Strindberg had a little experience in wild places, but the three of them had drawn up no plans for a march and had not practiced for one either. They hauled 300- and 400-pound sledges, when British sledgers, the best in the world, recommended 200 as a maximum, and Nansen's crewmember, having tried briefly to haul 250, said that a man might as well give up as make the attempt. And they managed it for nearly three months, wearing down all the while like watch-springs.

The assertion, not infrequently made, that Andrée lacked the courage to call the whole thing off is not, I think, accurate. There is no evidence that he cared how people regarded him. After returning from Spitsbergen in 1896 he made no remarks that suggested he felt compromised by what people thought of his courage, even though the papers compared him rudely to Nansen. Perhaps his force of will protected him from embarrassment—or the narrowness of his focus. He was a man who didn't put aside his plans if other people didn't agree with them.

I don't think he left because he was afraid not to. I think he left because he could no longer imagine not leaving. I think the desire to see if the balloon could do all that he was convinced that it could, plus the urge to discover the pole and settle the mystery of what was actually there, overpowered him, like a temptation one finally submits to. I think he couldn't have lived with himself if he had turned around, not because he would have questioned his nerve or his resolve or would have been self-conscious about facing people as Andrée-who-had-backed-down, but because, having had everything prepared and all obstacles dismantled, he wouldn't have been able to live peacefully without having taken the chance, without having stepped off into the unknown. Quietly, and without intending to, even while his attention was elsewhere, he'd undergone a species of conversion. Whereas he had first approached the task as a scientist, a disengaged engineer, aloof from the romance of the pole, he had become as zealous and wild-eyed as any fanatic who went off toward the unfound places. He had, in his way, been overtaken. To turn back might be to lose the chance forever, given how difficult it might have been to raise money for a third attempt, and the lost chance at the big deed is what I think he couldn't have borne. Certainly the expedition had collected its own momentum, but the part that I think pushed him forward was behind his eyes, not in front of them.

In the Andrée Museum in Gränna, where the relics of the expedition reside, there are three watches, one with a smashed dial, one stopped at 12:02, and one stopped at 7:31. In other cabinets are their clothes and many of their scientific instruments. Viewing stains on the side of the boat, one can imagine the gestures that might have caused them. There are cracks in the floorboards and the leather pieces, and knots that were tied by their hands.

There are photographs of the remains on tables in the examining room at the hospital. So little is left of one of them that he looks only like a collection of rags. Another has one leg. Both useless relics and the bodies of heroes, they lie in an unadorned room with a clawfoot tub in the background.

In another cabinet at the museum is a film can. On the side of the can is a notice from the manufacturer:

> A Suggestion. To avoid the possibility of allowing the film to grow old on your hands, paste the attached gummed slip in the front of your Kodak or on your roll holder. At least put it where it can be seen occasionally and can be readily referred to.
> —Eastman Kodak Company.
> Caution. This film should be used before January 1st, 1898.

The bulk of the rolls had been exposed, but ninety-three frames, taken mostly by Strindberg, were developed although many are only faintly legible.

Strindberg had a better than typical eye for composition—he had won a photography contest once. These were scientific men on a mission, though, and they weren't recording their moods or the scenery. Nevertheless there is a suggestion that Strindberg was taking note of a landscape that no one but they had ever seen, and the creatures that they encountered. Strindberg appears to have stopped taking photographs sometime before the end (there is no photograph of the icehouse, for example), suggesting that he could no longer bring himself to believe that he would live, or that the making of records of the trip became less important than the labor to survive.

One photograph shows Fraenkel and Andrée standing over a polar bear one of them had shot. The camera had a time exposure, so Strindberg was able to take a picture of the three of them trying to force a sledge through a gap in the ice. There is a photograph of a shot ivory gull with its wings spread and nailed to a plank, and of the fork that Andrée made from heavy wire for Fraenkel because the polar bear meat was often so tough that it bent the forks they had. The most desolate of the images was taken on July 14, when Strindberg walked about a hundred feet off on the ice and pointed the camera at the balloon, which was on its side, with the cab tipped over and Andrée and Fraenkel beside it. The black and white and the shades of gray within the photographs are weak and watery, and the figures insubstantial, leading everyone who sees them to think, They already look like ghosts.

72

After I got back from Sweden, I wondered what the Swedish Pavilion at the Centennial Exposition in Philadelphia had looked like, the one where Andrée had been the janitor. When I found a photograph of it I was astonished, because it was a building that I have passed nearly every day for almost twenty years. It was a tech-built house, the first, designed to replicate a Swedish country schoolhouse. After the fair it was taken down, and put up in Central Park, on the Upper West Side of Manhattan, near Seventy-ninth Street. For years it was a toolshed used by the park's gardener, and then it was a bathroom until a Swedish American citizens' organization objected. Since 1947 it has been a place where a puppet troupe gives performances and has its offices—it is called the Swedish Cottage Marionette Theatre.

From the outside the building probably looks more or less as it did in Philadelphia in 1876—dark-stained wood, with a certain amount of fancy scrollwork along the eaves. One of the two big rooms downstairs is the theater and, sitting there on a low bench, it is easy to imagine a tall, slender young man sweeping the floor, lost in thinking about the currents of the air and having no idea how he will die.

Acknowledgments

I am grateful to Caroline Zancan, at Alfred A. Knopf; Andrew Wylie and Jacqueline Ko at the Wylie Agency; Hakan Jorikson, at the Gränna Museum; and Katherine Stirling, Lila Byock, and Ann Goldstein at *The New Yorker*.

David Pearlman, who called himself Poppa Neutrino and was the subject of "The Happiest Man in the World," used to say thank you in a way that was so understated and humble that it conveyed a depth of gratitude that I have never heard the remark carry otherwise. In that spirit, I would like to say thank you to Jin Auh at the Wylie Agency, Ann Close at Alfred A. Knopf, and David Remnick at *The New Yorker* for their advice and judgment.

Rich Cohen, Charles McGrath, and Ian Frazier all helped me in one way or another make this book better. Willing Davidson helped me find Andrée's grave. I had a species of guardian angel in the person of a young man from Montana named Grant Baldridge, who lives in Stockholm and found things for me in Swedish libraries and translated them. This book couldn't have been written without his more than generous and intelligent help.

Bibliography

Adams, Percy G. *Travelers and Travel Liars, 1660–1800.* New York: Dover Publications, 1980.

Andersson, G. S. A. *Andrée: Hans följeslagare och hans polarfärd 1896–1897.* Stockholm: Norstedt, 1906.

The Andrée Diaries. London: Bodley Head Ltd., 1931.

Barrow, John. *A Chronological History of Voyages in the Arctic Regions Undertaken Chiefly for the Purpose of Discovering a North-East, North-West or Polar Passage Between the Atlantic and Pacific.* London: John Murray, 1818.

———. *Voyages of Discovery and Research Within the Arctic Regions from the Year 1880 to the Present Time.* London: John Murray, 1846.

Beattie, Owen, and John Geiger. *Frozen in Time: The Fate of the Franklin Expedition.* Vancouver: Greystone Books, 1987.

Berton, Pierre. *The Arctic Grail: The Quest for the Northwest Passage and the North Pole 1818–1909.* McClelland & Stewart, 1988.

Blake, E. Vale, ed. *Arctic Experiences, Containing Capt. George E. Tyson's Wonderful Drift on the Ice-Floe.* New York: Harper & Brothers, 1874.

Burke, Edmund. *A Philosophical Inquiry.* Oxford: Oxford University Press, 1988.

Capelotti, P. J. *By Airship to the North Pole.* New Brunswick, NJ: Rutgers University Press, 1999.

Dufferin, Frederick Temple Blackwood. *Letters from High Latitudes: Being an Account of a Voyage in 1856, in the Schooner Yacht "Foam" to Iceland, Jan Mayen, and Spitzbergen.* London: John Murray, 1887.

Ellis, Richard. *On Thin Ice.* New York: Alfred A. Knopf, 2009.

Fleming, Fergus. *Ninety Degrees North: The Quest for the North Pole.* New York: Grove Press, 2001.

Gosnell, Mariana. *Ice: The Nature, the History, and the Uses of an Astonishing Substance.* New York: Alfred A. Knopf, 2005.

Greenblatt, Stephen. *Marvelous Possessions: The Wonder of the New World.* Chicago: University of Chicago Press, 1999.

Bibliography

Guttridge, Leonard F. *Ghosts of Cape Sabine: The Harrowing True Story of the Greely Expedition.* New York: Berkley Books, 2000.

Haglund, Sven, and Anders Ångstrom. *Andrée: Mannen med vilja och mod.* Stockholm, 1930.

Hempleman-Adams, David, and Robert Uhlig. *At the Mercy of the Winds: Two Remarkable Journeys to the North Pole: A Modern Hero and a Victorian Romance.* London: Bantam Press, 2001.

Henderson, Bruce. *Fatal North: Adventure and Survival Aboard USS Polaris: The First U.S. Expedition to the North Pole.* New York: New American Library, 2001.

Jacobowsky, Carl Vilhelm. *Andrée: En man och en bragd.* Lund, Sweden, 1930.

Jung, C. G. *Aion: Researches into the Phenomenology of the Self.* Princeton: Princeton University Press, 1968.

Kane, Elisha Kent. *Arctic Explorations in Search of Sir John Franklin.* London: T. Nelson & Sons, 1885.

Kullenbergh, Carl I. *S. A. Andrée, hans lif och person: En skildring af vår stora Nordpolsfarare.* Göteborg, Sweden, 1898.

Lachambre, Henri, and Alexis Machuron. *Andrée's Balloon Expedition.* 1898.

Linder, Gurli. *S. A. Andrée: En levnadsteckning av,* Stockholm, 1909.

Loomis, Chauncey. *Weird and Tragic Shores: The Story of Charles Francis Hall, Explorer.* New York: Modern Library, 2000.

Lopez, Barry. *Arctic Dreams.* New York: Scribner, 1986.

Martinsson, Tyrone. *Nils Strindberg: En biografi om fotografen pa Andrées polarexpedition.* Lund, Sweden: Historical Media, 2006.

Maxtone-Graham, John. *Safe Return Doubtful: The Heroic Age of Polar Exploration.* London: Constable, 1988.

McClintock, Francis Leopold. *The Voyage of the "Fox" in the Arctic Seas: A Narrative of the Discovery of the Fate of Sir John Franklin and His Companions.* London: John Murray, 1859.

McGoogan, Ken. *Fatal Passage: The Story of John Rae, the Arctic Hero Time Forgot.* New York: Carroll & Graf, 2001.

Mirsky, Jeannette. *To the Arctic!: The Story of Northern Exploration from the Earliest Times.* Chicago: University of Chicago Press, 1970.

Moss, Sarah. *The Frozen Ship: The Histories and Tales of Polar Exploration.* New York: Bluebridge, 2006.

Nansen, Fridtjof. *In Northern Mists: Arctic Exploration in Early Times.* New York: Frederick A. Stokes, 1911.

———. *Farthest North: The Epic Adventure of a Visionary Explorer.* New York: Harper & Bros., 1897.

Pallin, H. N. *Andréegatan.* Uppsala, Sweden: J. A. Lindblads, 1934.

Putnam, George Palmer. *Andrée: The Record of a Tragic Adventure.* New York: Brewer & Warren, 1930.

Ransmayr, Christoph. *The Terrors of Ice and Darkness.* London: Weidenfeld & Nicolson, 1991.

Rolt, L. T. C. *The Aeronauts: A History of Ballooning, 1783–1903.* New York: Walker & Company, 1966.

Ryden, Per. *Den svenske Ikaros: Berättelserna om Andrée.* Stockholm: Carlssons, 2003.

Simmonds, P. L. *Polar Discoveries During the Nineteenth Century.* London: Routledge, Warne & Routledge, 1860.

Sollinger, Gunther. *S. A. Andrée: The Beginning of Polar Aviation, 1895–1897.* Moscow: Russian Academy of Sciences, 2005.

Spufford, Francis. *I May Be Some Time: Ice and the English Imagination.* New York: St. Martin's, 1997.

Stefansson, Vilhjalmur. *Unsolved Mysteries of the Arctic.* New York: Macmillan, 1938.

Sundman, Per Olof. *The Flight of the Eagle.* New York: Pantheon, 1970.

Thomas, David N. *Frozen Oceans: The Floating World of Pack Ice.* London: Firefly Books, 2004.

Wrakberg, Urban. *The Centennial of S. A. Andrée's North Pole Expedition.* Stockholm: Royal Swedish Academy of Sciences, 1999.

Wright, Helen S. *The Great White North: The Story of Polar Exploration from Earliest Times to the Discovery of the North Pole.* New York: Macmillan, 1909.

NEWSPAPER FILES

Boston Daily Globe
Chicago Daily Tribune
Guardian (Manchester)
New York Times
New York Tribune
St. Paul (MN) Globe
Salt Lake Herald
San Francisco Call
Times (London)
Washington Post

Illustrations

ALSO BY ALEC WILKINSON

"A beautiful, honest portrait."
–*Los Angeles Times*

THE PROTEST SINGER
An Intimate Portrait of Pete Seeger

A spirited and intimate look at American icon and activist Pete Seeger, and his life and his accomplishments. Pete Seeger transformed a classic American musical style into a form of peaceful protest against war, segregation, and nuclear weapons. Drawing on his extensive talks with Seeger, Alec Wilkinson delivers a first hand look at Seeger's unique blend of independence and commitment, charm, courage, energy, and belief in human equality and American democracy. We see Seeger, the child, instilled with a love of music by his parents; Seeger, the teenager, hearing real folk music for the first time; Seeger, the young adult, singing with Woody Guthrie. And finally, Seeger the man marching with the Rev. Martin Luther King in Selma, standing up to McCarthyism, and fighting for his beloved Hudson River. The gigantic life captured in this slender volume is truly an American anthem.

Biography

VINTAGE BOOKS
Available wherever books are sold.
www.vintagebooks.com